Uplifting

DEVOTIONALS

BOOK III

First Edition

Published by

HELPING HANDS
PRESS
www.myhelpinghandspress.com

ISBN: 978-1-62208-575-0

Printed in the United States of America

Contents

Connect with

Helping Hands Press

and all of their authors:

Website - MyHelpingHandsPress.com

Facebook – Facebook.com/HelpingHandsPress

Twitter - @HelpingHandsPre

Rooted

Finding God in the Gardens of Scripture
MURRAY PURA

The Garden Path

You have a cousin who's a Trappist monk – would you like to meet him?"

I was astounded. I was 25 years old before I found out I had a cousin who was a monk living in a monastery in the south end of the city. No one in the family had ever mentioned him. It was a mutual friend who figured it out. He set up a meeting and I showed up at the big iron gates and high walls of the monastery at the appointed time. I pulled a rope, a bell clanged, a figure cloaked in white and black came and greeted me and brought me inside to the Father Abbot.

I confess I was a bit apprehensive about meeting my cousin. After all, what did we have in common? He was Catholic, I was Protestant; he had taken a vow of chastity, I hoped to meet a young woman and get married; he spent his days isolated from the world in the monastery, I spent my days right in the middle of the world. For that matter, what did I have in common with any of the men who moved silently in and out of the abbot's office in black hoods and white robes?

But there was nothing to worry about. The abbot plied me with homemade cookies and glasses of fresh milk from the monastery's prize dairy herd – "Do you want another cookie? How about some more milk? What do you think of it, how does it taste, is it cold enough for you?" When my cousin finally arrived he was full of smiles and warmth and looked like Friar Tuck. Even though among themselves the Trappists maintained a vow of silence a large part of the time, with visitors they were allowed to speak freely. And laugh freely - which my cousin, Brother Martin, found very easy to do.

He took me on a tour of the monastery - down long stone corridors to the chapel, to the library, to the kitchen. We talked about family, about faith, about God. I told him about my work with a street church in the downtown area, and he exclaimed, "This is great, you're out there ministering to people and I'm in here praying for you!" The abbot popped up and gave me an old book on prayer by Francis de Sales. I talked to brothers who were milking the prize cows and who cracked jokes with me. The afternoon sped past and I was just heading out the gates when my cousin came running down the path calling my name: "Wait! Can you stay for supper? The brothers would love to have you as our guest!"

So I stayed on and ate fresh bread, drank more milk, helped myself to that great Trappist invention Oka cheese, had some pop, watched the young brothers eat and grin and pass bowls of salad back and forth along the long wooden table, and, after another hour or two, said my goodbyes and went home quietly in joy, one last time retracing my steps down the garden path to the front gates.

My cousin had walked me along that garden path where there were daisies and dill and long full rows of cabbage and lettuce and carrots and beets. Trappists are vegetarians so the garden is an important resource. It is not only one of the great essentials of their physical life, however, it is also critical for their spiritual sustenance: in the gardens they hoe and pray; in the gardens they walk and read Scripture; in the gardens they sit and meditate on God and worship.

Speckled by rain that summer Saturday, dark and green and unfolding, I was reminded as I walked the path that Christians had kept monasteries for almost 2000 years, and on and around the grounds of those monasteries they had grazed cattle, harvested grain and planted gardens of flowers, vegetables and herbs. The wonder was that this day, among a group of modern day monks, I had taken some of that growth into me and, in their company, nourished both my body and my spirit.

The Bible has its own garden path. It runs from Genesis to Revelation. In fact, some of the most important events in the Christian faith take place in Biblical gardens, events around which Christianity has established its doctrines as firmly as great rocks in the sand. Many of us have known these crucial teachings of the Christian faith since we were children – the fall into sin in the Garden of Eden, Christ's night of sorrow in the Garden of Gethsemane, his resurrection from dead at the Garden Tomb – yes, we know these teachings by heart.

Or maybe not by heart. How do the great teachings of Scripture get from our heads to our hearts and souls and make a difference to us in our ordinary lives? It is the gardens we find in the Bible that actually help those teachings hit home by bringing them down to earth – we can sift them through our fingers and bring them to our nostrils like good soil and smell in them the strength and health and vigor that bring the miraculous into our world.

Think about it. "God Almighty first planted a garden," writes Francis Bacon, who was born in 1561, "and, indeed, it is the purest of human pleasures; it is the greatest refreshment to the spirits of man."

God first planted a garden. He is given many names in the Bible - grand names, majestic names - but from the beginning to the end there is one name more illuminating than the rest which we can know him by: God is a gardener. In Genesis 2:8 we are told, "God planted a garden away to the east." Immediately we get an image of deity stooping down from the high heavens to dig out a hole in the ground for a maple sapling or an evergreen, eventually dropping to his knees to grub about in the soil. He is doing the things we do in gardens or we have seen others do: patting earth firmly around the base of a newly planted chokecherry bush, spreading the roots of a petunia, placing carrot seeds, watering. There is mud under his fingernails, mud under his skin, mud streaked under the sockets of his eyes. "The Lord God made trees grow up from the ground, every kind of tree pleasing to the eye and good for food". (v.9) I suppose you could say God did not get dirty at all, he simply spoke the garden into existence as Genesis 1 tells us: "God said, 'Let the earth produce growing things; let there be on the earth plants that bear seed, and trees bearing fruit each with its own kind of seed.' So it was." (Genesis 1:11)

I am hesitant, however, to interpret Genesis 1 as meaning that God is anything less than up close and personal with his creation. Yes, God does speak a great deal into existence, and declares many matters to be so, but then he goes about getting intimately involved in what he has just voiced. In Genesis 2 we are treated to a frame-by-frame playback after the big picture in Genesis 1. We no longer get a sense of God distant and transcendent in Genesis 2, so much as we get a sense of God hands-on with what he has made. God is bent over in the dust, on all fours, shaping a human out of the ground, placing divine lips over nostrils of dirt and breathing in the breath of life so that his sculpture of clay and mud becomes a living creature. (2:7) In Genesis 1 he says, "Let us make human beings in our image, after our likeness," (1:26) and in Genesis 2 he rolls up his sleeves and does it. Do we find that Genesis 2 tells us God merely speaks the garden into existence? No, we are told he plants it. How does the first human get into this garden? By a spoken command? No, God puts him there: "The Lord God took the man and put him in the garden of Eden to till it and look after it." (2:15) Our image of a gardening God with dirt up to his elbows and involved in his creation body and soul is not so whimsical after all, but the real thing.

And why not? What is the Son of God coming to earth, except deity taking on nostrils of dirt or legs and arms of dust? What is our salvation, but Christ planted dead in the ground like a seed and then bursting into life, cracking the crust of earth and night and bringing daybreak to the world? It's striking, isn't it, that Mary Magdalene, setting her eyes upon Jesus for the first time after the resurrection, thinks he's a gardener? (John 20:15) It's equally striking that the Bible goes full circle and ends where it begins, with a garden that God makes and in which humans live: "Now God has his dwelling with mankind! He will dwell among them and they shall be his people, and God himself will be with them . . . Then the angel showed me the river of the water of life, sparkling like crystal, flowing from the throne of God and of the Lamb down the middle of the city's street. On either side of the river stood a tree of life, which yields twelve crops of fruit, one for each month of the year". (Revelation 21:3, 22:1-2)

In the beginning, the Garden of Eden holds everything about the destiny and possibilities of human existence within its borders. The end of the Bible is that promise fulfilled in a second

Eden. The first Eden is like a seed, carrying all that is necessary for humans to co-exist in harmony with the earth and all that is upon it, including the divine being who fashioned the whole of it. The second Eden of heaven is the tree full grown without any danger of rot or disease or fire or flood bringing it down. But Eden in all its fullness is impossible without Eden in its infancy and fragility.

We know the story. The first Eden fell. But the spiritual Eden is with us still - it is the story of the entire human race and all of creation, all plants and animals and birds, all the sea and all the sky and all the glittering night. Because of the first Eden, the first garden, the Gardener will come to earth, clearly visible to all but unknown to most, and he will cause Eden to become what it was always meant to become: heaven on earth. How will he do this? The way all gardeners have it in them to restore a garden that has been overrun and reclaimed by the wild. He will weed. He will prune. He will replenish the soil. He will hoe and till. He will nurture it back to life so that the garden will unfold like a rose. Ultimately, he will water the soil with his blood. All this we would never experience except for the first Eden and the tragedy that drove humans from it. We would never know the lengths to which God would go to give us another life. We would never know how much he loved that race whose nostrils he had kissed and into whom he had breathed the air of his own immortality and inextinguishable light. "How great a Fall," wrote Augustine, "that merited so great a Redeemer."

The Bible is studded with references to sowing seed and growing crops and planting vineyards. But there are five passages that stand out – one in Genesis, one in the Song of Songs, two in the gospels, and a final one in the Revelation of John. They are the five gardens of God and the signs above their gates read: Eden, En Gedi, Gethsemane, the Garden Tomb and the garden of heaven, Second Eden. To walk through these gardens is to walk the garden path. And just like the monastic gardens they are much more than places where flowers and herbs grow. They are icons of the Father, Son and Holy Spirit, they are images of the transcendent, windows to heaven, metaphors of the spiritual life. Their roots must penetrate us and reach down into our very souls and the gardens themselves must be planted in us. Each one is a spiritual environment of such vitality and colour and wisdom that we need to enter them in prayer and meditation to seek God, to ask questions of the Gardener, to listen, to worship, to struggle, to be at peace. The Biblical gardens are a place of encounter with the Holy Spirit, "The Greening Power of God," as Hildegard of Bingen called him.

But the gardens are more than images and metaphors and symbols of the Christian faith. God's gardens are stories and these stories are all double-edged and triple-edged. They have meanings behind the obvious meanings. Trees may take on deeper significance. Fruit may stand for more than oranges or pears or grapes. Blood may be more than blood and do things ordinary blood cannot do. Animals may not be animals. Henna blossoms may not be henna blossoms. Death may not be death. Even the Maker of heaven and earth is known by different identities, a creator in one garden, a lover in another, a victim in yet another.

The Biblical gardens offer us stories that can take us "farther up and farther in" - the words Aslan spoke to encourage the boys and girls to plunge deeper into the mysteries and wonders of Narnia. As you stand among the gardens' trees and plants and bright waters and shadows you begin to feel that there was some truth to all of the fairy tales you were told when you were a child, all the stories about princes and princesses, about cunning sorcerers and powerful spells, all the tales of hidden jewels and towering castles and great creatures with flapping wings, all the fantasy epics that teem with flashing swords and enchanted gardens and talking beasts and thorns and thistles and banishment. You realize they were more than fantastical flights of the imagination. They were flights to the core of our existence. There is something in us that wishes to tell these stories and there is something in us that wishes to hear them. When these stories are told we relish the battle between good and evil, light and darkness, courage and cowardice, death and immortality.

Outwardly we may pretend to laugh off all the images of dark and light: "It's just a story". But inwardly we turn the themes of those childhood tales over and over in our minds and hearts. Before the dark of sleep. Gazing at a sunset that is a conflagration of cloud and flame. Silent in front of a blazing fire where the coals glitter like the stones of a magic palace. Alone at the stroke of midnight under the white stars of heaven. On a beach where the sea storm crashes into rock and sand and wind stings at your face and hands. No, the best fairy tales are not just stories. They are speaking about things that exist but they are speaking cryptically. They are in costume. We are not always certain what may be hidden behind the mask and colorful garments. Something is going on, but we can't quite get the whole of it. We reach out and grab onto bits and pieces. One part of the tale is about integrity. Another about deceit. That character embodies the sacred. This other character the unholy. The quest for the grail is a quest for the divine. The destruction of the Ring is the destruction of selfishness and lust and obsession, the vicious things we cling to and that cling to us. We come to believe that the greatest of these stories mean much more than they appear to mean on the surface, and that they represent deeper truths that are a part of our existence - truths seen and unseen.

In the Biblical gardens drops of sweat can turn into drops of blood, a dead man can come back to life. We do not just come to a rose bush or a peach tree when we come to God's gardens, but a whole world, physical, metaphysical, natural, supernatural, skin and bone and heart and spirit. Everything that matters is in these gardens, everything we feel—ecstasy, anguish—has a niche, everything that puzzles, all that inspires. The gardens are all of life and all of God.

There is one great difference between the fairy tales and the stories from the Bible however. The fairy tales show us things that are true, but the tales themselves are not real. Real persons do not get hurt. The evil in the fairy tales vanishes into air, into thin air. In the Bible, the stories are for real and real people do get hurt: women, children, men, even God. And the gardens in which so many stories take place are not illusions or special effects – they have real soil, real plants, real stones. The gardens are real and the people, the angels, the devils and the divine in them are real also.

As we look at these gardens together we will take each one as a whole. There may be a place for trying to figure out the symbolism of each plant or gardening tool used in the Bible, just as there may be a place for trying to nail down the hidden significance of every item and aspect of the tabernacle the children of Israel used in the desert—"Every natural fact," says Emerson, "is a symbol of some spiritual fact." We could say that when Isaiah talks about refashioning swords into plows, the plow is a symbol of opening soil rather than opening veins, and ought to be seen as God's call to peace. That shovels in Biblical stories stand for plantings, for spiritual beginnings, for cultivation, restoration and rejuvenation. A seed is spiritual possibility. It is also the tiniest amount of faith and a mustard plant symbolizes the miraculous growth of that small and slender hope. A Mexican friar, Emanuel de Villegas, described how each part of the passion flower symbolized something about the passion of Christ—the pointed leaves are the spear thrust into his side, the red styles the nails stained with his blood, and so on. If we took this approach to the five gardens of God we would soon be overwhelmed by a deluge of fragmentary information: some of it marginal, some of it absurd, some of it no doubt useful, but a good bit of it little more than smoke and mirrors. No, it is better that we come to the gardens seeking an atmosphere in which to think and pray and wonder, rather than one in which to play a Biblical Trivial Pursuit; to focus on God in his wholeness rather than the little bits and pieces, however bright and shining, that fall from his hands as he passes.

All we need to do is walk the garden path. Spend time in Eden, spend time in Gethsemane, stand still before an empty grave in a spring garden alive with honeybees and hummingbirds, yes, and alive with something much more. A day, an hour spent in these gardens can change a life and help us see what we may never have seen, or see it again, or see it in a way we never saw it before. And, if the light is right, see God in a way that we never saw him before. Perhaps the playwright George Bernard Shaw said it best, and though I think he said it with a smile, I think he also said it because he had been there and knew it was true: "The best place to find God is in a garden. You can dig for him there."

Eden
The Garden of Birth

"The Lord God planted a garden in Eden, away to the east."

Genesis 2:8

1

Rain slashed and wind cut and ocean waves thumped against the rocks and sand and stones. The night was cold and without stars, without moon, without light of any kind. Two men and a woman walked back and forth across a stretch of grass that sloped to the sea, hunched against the sting of the storm. A flashlight beam jumped up and down and illuminated shining grass and swinging trees. The wind seemed to grab the beam and hurl it from one side of the strip of land to the other. Out over the dark water was the chop of waves against boats and the snap of rigging against aluminum spars and the creak of cables pulling hard at their moorings. And farther out still the grunt and groan of a foghorn.

"You say it's two acres?" asked one of the men to the other. Water streamed down his glasses.

The man with the flashlight nodded. "From the highway right down to the cove."

"What about water?" asked the woman.

"You'll have to sink a well. But all the wells along this shore have sweet water. That's not a problem."

"The cove seems pretty sheltered even with this storm going on," said the man with the glasses looking out towards the ocean.

"Yeah, it would take a hurricane to really give you trouble tucked away in here."

"We'll take it then."

"You'll take it?"

The woman smiled and nodded, her hood and face wet with rain. "You bet we'll take it."

The man with the flashlight shook his head. "You walk around the property on the dirtiest night of the year, you can't see the hand in front of your face - why, it's like buying the place sight unseen."

They laughed - and began to walk up the grassy slope towards their cars as the wind and rain continued to pound on their heads and backs.

"You have a bunch of people waiting to see this property in the morning, am I right?" asked the man with the glasses.

"I sure do."

"We had to beat them to the punch."

"Well, you did that. Nobody else wanted to come out until after the storm had blown through. I'll have to call them all and tell them they can save themselves a trip."

"I guess you will."

The two men stopped by the cars and shook hands in the dark.

Once the storm had passed, the sun shone again and the sea glittered white and blue at the foot of the property like a net of gems. Over a period of weeks and months a well was drilled, a dock built and moored securely in the cove, a house erected and filled with furniture. But what the man and his wife had looked forward to most came in May – the opportunity to split open the grass and plant a garden.

Day after day their spades and picks cut apart the earth. Their mattocks and machinery turned the soil. They sweat and toiled and grunted and grinned. Halfway down the long slope of grass they planted a large vegetable plot. A strawberry patch was put there too. Near the plot they placed fruit trees. A grapevine. Raspberry canes. Dirt jammed under their fingernails and streaked black across their foreheads. Closer to the house they marked out flower gardens with orange, pink and purple petals. Roses. Herbs. They changed the land. They altered the colors of the earth. And they thought it was good, very good. So did many others.

When you change your world some things are diminished, some things are added. There was less grass on their property, though still plenty to go around, less white and red clover, less wide-open space. But the bees were in heaven, a heaven that had not existed for them before. Hummingbirds showed up, playing the air like a Stradivarius. Butterflies with pale blue wings arrived and rested on the highest daisies. Deer ate the lettuce, crows ate the corn. Robins came for worms. Blackbirds for berries. Chipmunks raided the feeding stations set up for sparrows and cardinals and nuthatches. Flies arrived also. But close on their wings came dragonflies of metallic green and emerald. Snakes without venom slid between flower stalks. Visitors made tea from fresh spearmint leaves. The gardens gave both humans and the creatures about them much pleasure. The gardens fed their bodies. Even with the hard work of weeding, the gardens offered a new happiness.

This was the garden of my wife's parents, Richard and Goldie, a garden built by the sea. Before their arrival, the waters of the Atlantic, for the most part, splashed against an untouched shoreline of earth and stone. For hundreds of years, thousands of years, the grass had not been turned. The soil had rested from generation to generation. The property looked perfect just the way it was— emerald field sloping down to rock and sand beach, trees tall, jade leaves, salt waters flashing as if the stars had fallen. But Richard and Goldie felt something was missing. Gardens. So they began to create them.

Not all gardens may be fenced. But all gardens have definite boundaries. There are edges to them, just as there are edges between sea and sky and land and ocean. They are separate from the world around them even though they haven't gone anywhere. A garden stands out. As lovely as the land around them might be, we notice gardens immediately: beauty within beauty.

It is in us to do what Richard and Goldie did. To plant. Create. Not only gardens of the ground, but gardens of the mind, of the spirit, gardens of music and gardens of words and gardens of worship. In all of these gardens I think, we are trying to find Eden again. Eden is an old memory we cannot recall except by glimpses of what our hands and imaginations do pretty much out of thin air, surprising us. "I never knew you had it in you," someone tells us while admiring our handiwork. Neither did we. The paint of Eden is in the violets and orchids we plant and admire. The music of Eden is in the melodies of the guitarist and the pianist and the cellist. The drama of Eden is in some of our finest plays and films. The sweetness we create. The symmetry. The prayers. The paradise. Something deep inside each one of us wants the first garden again. Something in us wants to re-create the world from scratch.

2

That first garden was perfection. In it was not only the possibility for the purest fulfillment of the human race but for all of creation. It was meant to be a paradise, which is, in fact, no different from saying it was meant to be a garden - both words mean the same thing. Our word paradise comes from the Greek paradeisos, garden, which comes from the Persian pairidaeza, an enclosed area, a wall around. Our English word garden finds its roots in the Old French jardin and the Old High German gart, both of which mean enclosure. So a garden is a place that is set apart, a place with unique boundaries, an area that is protected and distinct from that which is without. It's meant to be something special.

Why did God need to set aside such a place? The world was newborn, unpolluted, an expression of his own spirit and just as vital and fresh: "God saw all that he had made, and it was very good." (Gen. 1:31) There was no death or destruction, no violence, no nature red in fang and claw. Humans did not kill and eat. "Throughout the earth," God declares, "I give you all plants that bear seed, and every tree that bears fruit with seed: they shall be yours for food." (1:29) The animals and birds did not kill and eat either: "All green plants I give for food to the wild animals, to all the birds of the air, and to everything that creeps on the earth, every living creature." (1:30) In a way, the entire earth seemed to be a garden, rescued from being formless and empty and dark, a vast wasteland enclosed and transformed in a matter of days, a planet with a wall around that separated it from an environment in which humanity and other living creatures, plants, trees, and waters, could not survive. Earth itself became a garden in the galaxy.

Yet God still chose to plant a special garden amidst all this goodness. God created the first person, then made the garden, and then placed the person in the garden to till it and look after it. A river had its source in Eden, it watered the garden and then split into four, only two rivers of which we can identify with certainty - the Tigris and the Euphrates.

It is in the garden that the first human experiences companionship with the creatures God has made, at least all those not confined to the seas: "Then the Lord God said, 'It is not good for the man to be alone; I shall make a partner suited to him.' So from the earth he formed all the wild animals and all the birds of the air, and brought them to the man to see what he would call them." (2: 18, 19) The animals we enjoy as our companions today are a link to that Edenic experience, and we take as much enjoyment out of naming them as the first man presumably did. There was no fear or estrangement between the creatures of the air and the land and humanity at this point. They were all in it together, in this special garden within a garden, this goodness within goodness.

What sort of picture do we come up with for this first garden of all gardens? For many of us, a picture so extraordinary that Eden may seem like an illusion or a fantasy, something completely impossible, a place that could never exist except in our wildest dreams – no animal hurting another, no fighting, no bloodshed, no cruelty between man or beast in the whole wide world.

But perhaps we are supposed to see Eden in the light of the fantastic. After all, isn't this the work of the beyond-what-you-can-ask-or-imagine Gardener, a garden unrestricted by killing frosts or marauding tigers or global warming? Isn't Eden meant to represent an idyllic existence? What else is a cow striking up a friendship with a bear, or a leopard lying down with a baby goat, or, for that matter, bats and dragonflies relaxing with gnats and mosquitoes? Isn't that the image of the perfect world Isaiah offers us? (Isaiah 11) Isn't that the image of the world as it was meant to be that Eden offers us? Surely the God of the platypus and ostrich and giraffe is a God of visions and dreams and, if so, visions and dreams are an essential aspect of Eden and the Edenic. Whether we are capable of picturing it or not, everything was in the garden, including man and woman, and everything had a name and it all fit.

3

A year after we were married my wife and I moved to the city of Vancouver in Canada. We rented a basement suite that had a backyard patio. The small bit of yard beside the patio was no more than a tangle of tall grass and weeds and rocks. That spring our landlords asked if we wanted to make a garden out of it and Linda and I agreed to give it a try. I bought and devoured books on gardening. We learned how to double-dig so that the soil became a dark flour. We went down two feet or more. We yanked pop cans out of the ground. Plastic containers. Rusty spikes. I pried up boulders that I staggered around the patio with. My landlord hauled them across the street and dropped them into English Bay where and they were no longer covered by dirt but by the waters of the Pacific.

Once the soil was ready we began to sprinkle tiny seeds into wide furrows. I remember thinking as the seeds fell—and I still think this every time I do it—"How can anything come out of these things? They are so small and they look so dead." We wielded trowels and made a bed for tomato plants. Sunflower seeds went into the mix. The west coast sun warmed the earth, water from the hose made rain.

Every morning before work we took a look. Nothing. Until the radishes came up all in a hurry, shouldering the earth aside and going for air. No radishes tasted better. Tomatoes rounded and ripened though I did have to put a couple of dozen inside a dark cupboard to finish the process. The sunflowers must have thought they were from magic seeds. They grew and grew and grew up to the second floor and peeked in our landlords' bedroom window. My wife and I were both amazed. So were our landlords.

But as beautiful as it was to us, it was far from the paradise of Eden. Our garden didn't stay perfect. Worms ate into our radishes as well as massive slugs—some green, some black, some leopard-spotted, antennae up, sliding like aliens over the landscape. Cats stepped on everything, obviously not willing to relinquish a favorite trysting spot just because we had turned it into trim rows of vegetables and herbs. Still, the garden survived. And because it did, many an hour was spent with friends sitting in the backyard, talking and sipping lemonade and watching honeybees and monarch butterflies and the red robins who hopped between plants, cocked their heads, and cracked the earth with their beaks.

So we brought a garden into the world that had never existed before, just as Linda's parents had done years before in Nova Scotia.

The garden did not take over the world. It was just a very small and wonderfully new part of it. True to its name, the garden had its definite boundaries beyond which it could not go—a neighbor's fence, white patio stones, the back wall of the cedar house. Yet it brought peace and life and pleasure that were unique to that space. Where there are been chaos, it brought order. Where things had been grim, it brought good cheer to a backyard that had been bleak and uninviting. Thus are gardens supposed to do. Even imperfect ones. And, as stories go, we know what happened to Eden's garden – it did not stay perfect either.

4

Like watching the kind of film where all the beauty and happiness of the first hour disintegrates in the second, like a tragedy written by the Greek playwrights or by Shakespeare or by Job, like a bad dream that doesn't vanish when you wake up: Eden falls into ruins.

And with it falls everything. Indeed, here is where the headwaters of all human tragedy rise like a flood. Eden is the crux of the human dilemma: Why is a human existence which is so permeated with pleasure also so violated by suffering and death? A peaceful garden, a sweeping green that causes a rush to the heart, a golden light slanting over bright flowers and vivid leaves—every summer we experience this beauty -why must it be so transient? Why is it impossible to stay in that garden, body and soul? Why is it only a glimpse, a moment, something given that swiftly becomes something lost? Why does the frost kill it? Why does the frost kill us?

In the middle of the garden God has planted a choice. When all is said and done it comes down to trust. Whose words matter? Whose voice? Man and woman go beyond God's words and in so doing they go beyond God. They reach outside of the enclosure. They violate the embrace. Eden recurs throughout the history of the human race and one of the ways in which it recurs is the choosing of generation after generation to go beyond the words of God and the garden wall. What God meant to be special is seen as a trap and a restriction, a denial of freedoms and rights and pleasures. The grass is lush on the other side. We're sure of it. The illusion is that outside of God and his words and his love is where a person finds what matters and what is sweet. The reality that is inevitably discovered is the reality which became that of the man and the woman of Eden: life outside the garden is no garden. It is exile.

The snake, forever marked as the one that starts the fall into ruin is not in and of itself evil. We must remember that snakes too were part of the "very goodness" of creation in Genesis 1. Man, "imago dei", named it and was not estranged from it. Moses made a bronze snake, at God's command, and lifted it up on a pole so that anyone who had been bitten by a poisonous snake would recover. (Numbers 21:8, 9) This image of the snake on the pole, Nehushtan, remains today a symbol used by the medical profession to symbolize healing. It will also become an image of Christ and the cross and so a symbol of divine redemption: "Just as Moses lifted up the snake in the desert, so the Son of Man must be lifted up, that everyone who believes in him may have eternal life." (John 3:14, 15 NIV) Moreover, the day when God's Kingdom rules on earth, Isaiah tells us, "The infant will play over the cobra's hole, and the young child dance over the viper's nest." (Isaiah 11:8) When Eden returns to earth, the snake will be a friend of children, much as my son and daughter in their younger years lifted garter snakes from the creek behind our house, held them without fear, then returned them to the water gently and without hate.

Clearly the snake or serpent in Eden is controlled by another force. God is squaring off against something more than snakes when he pronounces judgment within the garden: "I shall put enmity between you and the woman, and between your offspring and hers; he will crush your head, and you will strike his heel." (Gen. 3:15 NIV) It is seen by many as a prophecy about Christ, that the adversary possessing the snake, a being later to be known as Satan (the name means "adversary" in Hebrew) will come into conflict with the Son of God, born of a woman, and will be defeated.

There is a curious passage in Ezekiel that is supposed to be about the majesty and arrogance of the King of Tyre but which, like the passage about the snake in the garden, seems to hold a double meaning: "You were in Eden, the garden of God . . . You were anointed as a guardian cherub, for so I ordained you. You were on the holy mount of God; you walked among the fiery stones. You were blameless in your ways from the day you were created till wickedness was found in you . . . So I drove you in disgrace from the mount of God, and I expelled you, O guardian cherub, from among the fiery stones." (Ezekiel 28:13-16, NIV)

The King of Tyre was no guardian cherub; he was never in Eden. But another was - a cherub who fell from grace, a being of great pride and sparkling beauty - one who became for those who were in the image of God, the voice of God.

Whether the man and woman fully realized the choice they were making, both of them were subordinating God's words to the words of another. There was a contradiction about what God had said or not said and they chose to go with the one who voiced the contradiction. The man knew as well as the woman what kind of fruit he was biting into. He recognized it. He had seen it hanging from the tree in the middle of the garden, the tree of the knowledge of good and evil. It looked good. It tasted good. It was the thing to do: they could not only be in the image of God, they could be God. It seemed to be such a win-win deal. So they ate the fruit that gave the knowledge of good and evil, the fruit they thought would bring life to the fullest. And in so doing, died.

The garden does not change. They change. Now they see nakedness. Now they hide their bodies. Now they hide from God. The Gardener, like any gardener, strolls about in his garden in the pleasant coolness of the evening of a warm day, examining his flowers and plants and shrubs, expecting his children, made in his image, to join him and enjoy the stroll with him as they have always done. But the relationship is broken between parent and child. The freedom to be unafraid in God's presence and to be intimate with him is gone.

A moment later, we see that the relationship between humanity and the animal kingdom is also broken as, first of all, the woman accuses the snake, and later, as God slays an animal and uses the skin to clothe the woman and man. (3:13:21) The first blood is shed on earth. It signifies an alienation of stunning magnitude: between humanity and nature as well as humanity and God - even alienation between God and nature since God never intended his living creatures to be killed for food or clothing. The break between humans and nature is reinforced by God's words to the man: "On your account the earth will be cursed. You will get your food from it only by labor all the days of your life; it will yield thorns and thistles for you. You will eat the produce of the field, and only by the sweat of your brow will you win your bread until you return to the earth" (Genesis 3:17—19) There is even a chasm of pain that opens up between a woman and her own body, her own womb, in childbirth, and another that yawns wide and makes a woman subordinate to a man. (3:16) The harmony of Eden is rapidly unraveling.

It gets worse. Man and woman are driven from the garden and denied immortality. God settles them to the east of Eden, but to ensure they do not desecrate the garden again, or take what is not theirs to take, cherubim and a fiery sword that flashes and whirls block off the tree of life. Humans will never be the gods they imagined they could be. Twice they are denied life by angels: once in the garden, by a winged being disguised as a serpent, and again at the gate to the garden, by an angelic being in full view with outspread wings and a sword that burns but is not consumed. (Ezekiel 41:19, Gen. 3:24) The Gardener is holy and his garden is holy. But humans no longer are.

The tragedy will be compounded. There will be a first-born, a son, and he will murder his younger brother, and human blood will soak into the dust humanity was formed from, mingling with the blood of animals killed not only for clothing and food but also for sacrifice. (Gen. 4:1-10) Not only will murder continue, but pride and gloating in being a murderer. (Gen. 4:23) Vengeance will come. (4:24) Wickedness will increase from generation to generation until God will wish humans had never been born. The earth and the animals that were once in such unity in Eden are at war with each other and humanity - and when God punishes human wickedness, they will suffer along with women and men: "I shall wipe off the face of the earth this human race which I have created—yes, man and beast, creeping things and birds. I regret that I ever made them" (Genesis 6:7).

But we take note that Evil is not birthed in Eden. It already exists. That is why there could be a tree that offered knowledge of it. God's idea was to form humanity in his image, but keep it safe from evil within the enclosure. Yet to stay within God's garden or not was, in the end, a choice that the first humans would be allowed to make, and in order for it to be a true choice, there needed to be a true option. The temptation was permitted, the Adversary allowed to be at large, "ranging over the earth from end to end", and be the Tempter (Job 1:7). Human life – even more, the life of the entire earth - was meant to be other than it presently is. Genesis tells us the reason we no longer experience Eden is not because God forced a sinful humanity from the garden. We left it the moment we looked to someone other than God, and, the truth is, we continue to leave it, of our own free will, every time we look past him for life.

5

When I was a boy I grew up in a neighborhood where just about everyone had a garden, small or large, and not just of flowers: raspberries, strawberries, carrots, tomatoes, potatoes, corn . . . you name it, our neighborhood grew it all. But there was one gardener who grew everything just a little bit sweeter, a little bit taller, a little bit better. He used trellises, he used poles, he used yards and yards of hose, he even used mirrors to reflect sunlight, and his garden filled the yard and touched the sky. My friends and I called him Mister Buon Giorno, Mister Good Morning, because he came from Italy and he had such a warm and sunny bright-new-morning disposition.

Every summer we all planted our gardens and every summer his vegetables and fruit trees soared while ours merely inched their way above the soil line. And every harvest he gave extra apples and plums and potatoes away to others. We would often see him sitting in the middle of his garden in July, sipping a glass of water, totally relaxed, watching his plants thrive. I would often run down the back lane past his yard and I always felt I was racing by some sort of jungle greenhouse without a roof or walls. His garden was like a great green thumbprint among our lawns and houses and cement sidewalks and asphalt streets.

But the years went by and in time he grew ill and could not care for his garden as he once had and it began to fall apart. Support poles broke, trellises sagged, trees withered, weeds spread. When he died the garden died with him. His wife moved away and the new owners cared nothing for what he had planted and tirelessly nurtured. They seeded the garden plot and Mister Buon Giorno's Little Eden vanished under a thick carpet of Kentucky bluegrass. Yet even though all traces of its glory is gone, you never forget a garden like that or the man who created it. Like God, we look on such beauty and pronounce it good. It in turn plants something of itself in us that may take root and give life long after it has vanished from the earth.

If the Biblical Eden is both a garden of birth and a garden of death it is also a garden of grace. There are many gardens and many stories that follow it and none of them would have been possible if God had not chosen to remain in relationship with his fallen creation—humans, birds, animals, fish and whales and giant squids, all flora and all fauna. Before Adam and Eve leave Eden, God permits the death of one of his animals so that they can be warm and adequately covered for the harsher existence ahead of them. The woman acknowledges that, "With the help of the Lord I have brought into being a male child." (Gen. 4:1) The ability to create human life reflects the work of God in creating human life. It is a great gift that is not destroyed by the fall. It survives. So does the coming together of man and woman. (Gen. 2:24) One of the great blessings of the fall, in fact, is the development of sexuality or becoming one flesh. It is no longer simply for companionship that Adam and Eve enjoy intimacy, but in exile from the garden their relationship with one another becomes the means of procreation. When the Adam is 130 years old Eve births him "a son in his own likeness, in his own image" and names him Seth, which means "granted". As if the wish of the human race to remain in existence and to keep the image of God that is their essence will be honored.

Perhaps one of the greatest surprises of the biblical story is that imago dei (the image of God in humans) is never extinguished. Even more surprisingly, despite the ups and downs and wicked twists of humanity, neither is God's desire to live in intimacy with men and women—"He will dwell among them and they shall be his people, and God himself will be with them." (Revelation 21:3) God, undying Gardener and Nurturer that he is, has not relinquished the dream and vision of another Eden where unity between himself and what he has made - all that he has made - will be restored. His quest for a second Eden is all-consuming. Just as that same quest for paradise, for all the wrong turns it has taken, is all-consuming for the human heart. Not only will there be a garden at the end of the world, just as there was at the beginning, there will be many lesser gardens and oases along the way to refresh and reinvigorate the human spirit and to keep the hope alive. Eden is a symbol of what will be again and of what was always meant to be.

6

Between the first Eden and the second Eden hangs the rest of the Bible and all of human history. We do not see this because we often do not see the significance of the first Eden to begin with. Genesis has become a battleground of creationists and evolutionists. Of those who say it is legend and those who say it is literal. Of those who claim the truth within is the truth of a parable, while others claim it is the truth of a proposition—the facts presented are either true or false exactly as they stand. What is missed about Eden in particular is its essence: God created all life and he wants to be intimate with it, close to it, especially with humanity, created so lovingly in his image. The thrust is that no matter who argues how it was done, God did it—not blind forces, not uninitiated chemical reactions, not a haphazard design with no intelligence behind it, not Nature without a Creator. Eden is a divine beginning. And to bring it back, which God fully intends, it will take nothing short of a divine restoration.

I wonder if too much emphasis is laid on the tragic end of Eden and too little on the beauty that existed at its beginning. Every good thing we experience is a reminder of the garden that was and the garden that will be again. Marriage, for example, is both an echo of the first Eden and the whisper of the coming Eden. Man and woman are united for the first time in the original Eden: Genesis tells us, "That is why a man leaves his father and mother and attaches himself to his wife, and the two become one." (Genesis 2:24) After the fall, marriage continues to allow man and woman to experience something of the perfect unity that existed between them in the garden. In the second Eden, there will, at last, be true unity between them and their God. Jesus tells us there will no longer be marriage as we know marriage now, but closeness between men and women will exist to a greater degree than was possible before - they will be like "angels in heaven" (Matthew 22:30), intimacy with one another in a new kind of wholeness, as well as intimacy with God.

Even outside of the marriage relationship friendship between humans is also both an echo of the unity that existed in the first Eden and the rumor of a second Eden where all the good that happened in the first garden will happen again. So is friendship between animals and humans. So is the unlikely but not impossible friendship between typical enemies in the animal kingdom. So is harmony, rather than violence and exploitation, between humans and the natural environment.

Every newborn reminds us of our birth in Eden, of our birth after Eden and the continuation of the image of God in humans, and also of our new birth into the Eden that is to come, where there will be no more death or suffering. (Revelation 21:4) Everything that approaches the oneness and well-being and peace on earth God intended at the start and still intends is nothing short of Edenic. And all that is Edenic is the great desire of God.

Recently, my wife mentioned to me that the symbol for the Holy Spirit in the ancient Irish Church was not the dove, it was the wild goose. This seems right and true. When the wild geese come north and bring spring with them it is the Holy Spirit coming too, bringing Eden and all the gardens of Eden in his wings. The wild geese are the coming of God. And if those geese are a metaphor for divinity, Eden and gardens are no less a metaphor for divinity and the human soul.

So Eden ought to be an encouragement to us. Its beauty is not lost. Like the coming of spring and the return of the wild geese, we will see it once more. We will experience it to the roots of our beings. It is a symbol of the sacred enclosure and that sacred enclosure is the loving and encircling embrace of God. If we respond to God's love we are within that embrace, we are within that garden. For the garden is not only a pleasure that will occur, it is a present reality of the human spirit for all who wish to live in relationship with their Creator and Redeemer.

Jesus walked through two gardens, Gethsemane and the Garden Tomb, to make the second Eden a powerful hope, and to open the gate to an ever-present garden of the heart. Those who believe and pray, they know something of the garden of the heart, they know something of Eden. Those who worship the living God, they know something of the garden of the heart, they know something of Eden. Those who pick up their cross and follow Jesus, those who lay down their lives for the gospel, those who give cups of cold water to the little ones, they know something of the garden of the heart, they know something of Eden. As long as we live, those of us who believe have a garden of the heart. It never vanishes. No matter what weeds sprout in it or which thistles attempt to choke it. It is a planting of God. It is the circle of his arms. One day it will not only be within and uncluttered, it will be all around us, untainted and unending.

The garden of the heart is the one garden that cannot be lost and it contains all the other gardens within its embrace. We lose some of the gardens in our lives, don't we? We have all known peace and pleasure and we have had our peace and pleasure shattered. We have experienced unity with others only to see that unity break apart. We have known intimacy with God and we have lost intimacy with God. Relationships with friends, with children, marriages, we have seen all of this wonder come to an end in our lives or in the lives of others. We have known Eden and we have known what it is to be outside of Eden, barred from its peace. We have suffered. We have wept. We have felt we had nothing to live for.

Yet we know something of what we have lost. We have experienced bits and pieces of what is good and right and we know good and right exist. Even if it seems we cannot find it again, no matter how hard we try or how hard we pray, we know it is there. We were in Eden once, if only for a few moments or hours or years. Yesterday we were there. The gardens of the Bible tell us we will come back inside it again. The gardens we plant with our minds and our hands tell us. The garden of the heart tells us. One day Eden will fill our soul, fill all our senses, fill our entire world.

I once lost a dog that had been my constant companion for almost 15 years. I went with him and his mate on well over ten thousand walks and traveled literally over ten thousand miles through cities and forests and mountain ranges and along the shores of the sea. In all moods I walked, whether I was living or dead, up or down, close to God or far, hopeful or fearful. I talked to that dog constantly. But our real communication was done with touch - through the emotions I voiced or did not voice, in silence as I lay beside him, or the long looks into the eyes. When he died pain roared through me like a storm surge. I felt I had been violated and beaten and left in a ditch of stones. I had known friendship with another creature. I had known a harmony that was meant to exist. I had known a great happiness that made me feel like a nine year old boy. And I had lost it all and lost him.

A few hours after he died, I went to a window in my house and looked out as I had looked out hundreds of times. I knew why I was there. I was hoping to see him. I was hoping I had somehow been mistaken and that he was still alive. I stood there a long time, praying and waiting. A voice inside me asked, "What are you looking for, Murray?" And I answered without thinking: "I am looking for Eden."

What I experienced with Yukon had been Edenic. Inside, I had known this. I had relished every minute of the relationship, all the months, all the days. How many years had I expected it to continue? Sixteen? Seventeen? Twenty? I knew the answer to that as well—forever.

We lose parents. We lose children. We lose brides and bridegrooms. We lose animal companions. We lose beautiful vistas and beautiful dreams. We even lose ourselves. Yet we know Eden when we see it, even if sometimes we see it after it is over, and that sense of place, that sense of paradise gained and paradise lost, that sense of grief, to me is a proof of the truth of the story. And if the first story is true all the other stories caught up in it must be also. This is the hope the first garden gives us. That the stories of God are the true stories of the world and that he will plant another garden for us, another Eden away to the east, and put us in it.

Taking a Walk with Jesus

TRACY KRAUSS

GOD WITH US EVERYDAY

And behold, two of them were going that very day to a village named Emmaus, which was about seven miles from Jerusalem. And they were conversing with each other about all these things which had taken place. And it came about that while they were conversing and discussing, Jesus Himself approached and began travelling with them.
Luke 24: 13 – 15

God meets with us in the everyday, ordinary experiences of our lives. Often we don't even recognize that we've had a 'God moment' until much later. Sure he can meet us during the 'big events' too, but more often than not, He wants to meet with us during our day-to-day life. In the passage above, two men were on a road trip, travelling from Jerusalem to Emmaus, which was about seven miles. At first that doesn't sound very far, but remember, they were on foot. While they walked, they were talking about the latest 'news', namely Jesus' crucifixion.

I want you to think for a moment about times in your life when God met with you in simple, everyday ways. We tend to over look these moments, but I believe that God can speak to us profoundly through our everyday experiences. I've moved more times than I have digits and I've lived in some very remote places. Each time, God was faithful in providing just the right housing, just the right job, at the just the right time. I've experienced times of poverty and I've also had times of plenty. From flat tires on deserted dirt highways, to getting stranded on the tundra in the middle of polar bear season, I've had a few adventures, too. God brought me through each one of these but He's also been there during the mundane and ordinary. Allow God to speak to you each day through the highs and the lows.

IT WAS HIM ALL THE TIME

But their eyes were prevented from recognizing Him. And He said to them, "What are these words that you are exchanging with one another as you are walking?"
And they stood still, looking sad. And one of them, named Cleopas, answered and said to Him, "Are you the only one visiting Jerusalem unaware of the things which have happened here in these days?"
Luke 24: 16-18

Sometimes, like Cleopas and his friend, we don't realize God is doing anything until much later. In this passage it says that they were prevented from recognizing Him, obviously for a greater purpose later on. However, we often choose not to see God's hand in our lives.

Back in the nineties, my husband and I ran the Youth Group at our church. I think back to some of the stuff we did with them and I cringe. Some of our activities weren't that spiritual and we basically blundered along just doing the best we knew how. Several years later, we were at a conference for pastors in Banff. We were surprised to meet up with a young man who had been in our youth group almost ten years earlier. He came from a particularly troubled background, and we doubted at the time that he was even getting anything out of YG. However, there he was at the conference, thanking us. He said our unconditional acceptance was what brought him to Christ and ultimately led him into ministry.

I know you've had experiences like this, too. Often it's the seemingly unimportant things that have the biggest impact. All our planning cannot take the place of God appointed opportunities. 1 Samuel 15: 22 says, "Obedience is better than sacrifice." Just do it and let God sort out the details.

Excerpted from *LIFE IS A HIGHWAY – Advice and Reflections On Navigating the Road of Life.* Copyright Tracy Krauss 2013.

Scripture references from the NEW AMERICAN STANDARD BIBLE, copyright 1960, 1962, 1963, 1968, 1971, 1972, 1973, 1975, 1977, 1995 by the Lockman Foundation. Used with permission.

GOD'S AGENDA ISN'T OUR AGENDA

And He said to them, "What things?"
And they said to Him, "The things about Jesus the Nazarene who was a prophet, mighty in deed and word in the sight of God and all the people, and how the chief priests and our rulers delivered Him up to the sentence of death, and crucified Him. But we were hoping that it was He who was going to redeem Israel. Indeed, besides all this, it is the third day since these things happened.
Luke 24: 19-21

Can't you just hear the disappointment? Have you ever felt that way – 'disappointed' in God? We all have our own agenda - our own hopes and expectations about how life should go. This includes our marriage, job, children - even how life should be once we accept Jesus. Here's a wake up call. More often than not, our agenda isn't the same as God's.

This is true even when our agenda seems godly and good. In the above passage, Cleopas and his friend were hoping that Jesus was the Messiah; that He would save Israel and release them from the overbearing rule of the Roman Empire. Their 'agenda' lined up with prophetic scripture and notice how they even quote Jesus himself. "It is the third day," they said. They obviously were remembering that Jesus said He would rise on the third day. To them it didn't look like Jesus had fulfilled his promises. Instead, it looked like God had messed up.

Understandably, they were disappointed. Of course they were! Does that mean they were bad people? No. Their plans were good plans - godly plans. They even seemed to line up with scripture. Yet God's way of fulfilling His promise was totally different than what they had expected.

It could be the same way for you, today. You might have a lot of plans that are good and godly and maybe you even feel like you've had confirmation from God through scripture or some other divine appointment. Just remember, no one can put God in a box.

Excerpted from *LIFE IS A HIGHWAY – Advice and Reflections On Navigating the Road of Life*. Copyright Tracy Krauss 2013.

GOD IS AT WORK EVEN WHEN WE DOUBT

But also some women among us amazed us. When they were at the tomb early in the morning and did not find His body, they came saying that they had also seen a vision of angels who said that He was alive. And some of those who were with us went to the tomb and found it just exactly as the women also had said, but Him they did not see."
Luke 24: 22-24

I can see myself in this scripture and maybe you can, too. You see, even 'believers' have doubts. The men in this passage didn't believe the testimony of others, but needed to see Jesus with their own eyes.

I've seen a lot of 'stuff' in my time as a believer: miracles, healings and people getting touched by the Holy Spirit. I've felt the power of God in my own life and I've witnessed it first hand in the lives of others.

And yet ... AND YET... I still doubt. Sometimes when I hear a fantastic testimony, my first reaction is to doubt. Come on now! You've been there, right? Someone says, we're praying for revival in 'Your Town', for example, and we might smile and 'pray' along – or should I say 'play along' - but do we really believe?

What about when someone you know gets cancer or another horrible sickness? Of course we pray, but do we really believe for healing? Now, I want to caution you here. I know of a pastor whose wife had cancer and he prayed fervently for her healing, as he should. Many of his congregation did the same, and they were convinced that she was going to be healed.

And then she died. It split the church. It devastated him to the point where he left the ministry and floundered in his faith. Their kids turned away from God. It was a horrible situation.

We want to have the kind of faith that moves mountains, but we must also remember that God's ways aren't our ways. He knew exactly what he was doing when Jesus died and rose again and He knows exactly what He is doing in your life today. He sees the bigger picture.

Excerpted from *LIFE IS A HIGHWAY – Advice and Reflections On Navigating the Road of Life.* Copyright Tracy Krauss 2013.

Strengthen Your Faith
Through the Word and Fellowship

*And He said to them, "O foolish men and slow of heart to
believe in all that the prophets have spoken! Was it not
necessary for the Christ to suffer these things and to enter
into His glory?" And beginning with Moses and all the
prophets, He explained to them the things concerning Himself
in all the scriptures.*

Luke 24: 25-27

Everything we need for life and instruction - God's
roadmap, if you will - can be found in scripture. Sometimes it
isn't that obvious, however, and takes some digging and even
some instruction. This is why I believe it is so important to get
plugged into a God fearing, scripturally sound church family.

I know people that feel content to 'do church' at home in
front of their TV, or who feel they don't need a church because
they can read the Bible for themselves. While that may be true,
there is something important about getting together with other
believers to discuss the scriptures. It's what Jesus does in this
passage. Cleopas and his friend probably knew the scriptures
but Jesus expounded and explained it to them, increasing their
insight and understanding.

Being part of a church also keeps us accountable. While
there are lots of ways to get solid Bible teaching online and
elsewhere, meeting face to face is important because we need
each other. Human beings are naturally social in nature. We
need the fellowship of like-minded people. Whole books have
been written on the benefits of the 'body', so it is not my intent
to go into all aspects here. The Word itself sums it up by
saying, "Do not forsake the assembling of yourselves together."

Get together and get into the Word!

Excerpted from *LIFE IS A HIGHWAY – Advice and
Reflections On Navigating the Road of Life.* Copyright Tracy
Krauss 2013.

EVERYONE NEEDS A REVELATION

And they approached the village where they were going and He acted as though He would go farther. And they urged Him saying, "Stay with us, for it is getting toward evening and the day is now nearly over." And He went in to stay with them. And it came about that when He had reclined at the table with them, He took the bread and blessed it, and breaking it, He began giving it to them. And their eyes were opened and they recognized Him; and He vanished from their sight.
Luke 24: 28-31

I find this an interesting reference to the Lord's supper. It was something Jesus not only instituted before his death, but afterwards as well. The thing that really jumps out at me, though, is the verse that says, "Their eyes were opened and they recognized Him." These travelers had what I like to call a 'revelation experience'.

Hopefully, you have had a 'revelation' experience of your own - that moment in time when your eyes were opened and you saw Jesus for who He is - your Lord and Savior. If you haven't had that, I urge you to seek out a Christian friend.

Notice that the revelation experience is often preceded by much preparation. In this case, Cleopas and his friend had been around Jesus for quite some time. We know this because earlier in this same passage, it is implied that they were followers, perhaps for up to three years during His ministry on earth. But it wasn't until they had walked, discussed, doubted, and listened to Jesus explaining the scriptures that their eyes were opened and they recognized Him. They had a revelation experience.

I think this is an important passage for those of us that are already believers, as well. It offers a measure of relief. You see, I don't consider myself to be an evangelist, and I've felt guilty at times for not witnessing to others like I should. (Or at least like I'm made to *feel* I should by well meaning folks who *are* evangelists.) The good news is, I'm not the one saving people! It's not my great testimony, my knowledge of the Bible, or how well I can debate. The fact is, it's about God's timing. It's the Holy Spirit who 'opens the eyes' of an individual. Although each Christian has a part to play in leading others to Christ, ultimately it is up to God.

Excerpted from *LIFE IS A HIGHWAY – Advice and Reflections On Navigating the Road of Life*. Copyright Tracy Krauss 2013.

Scripture references from the NEW AMERICAN STANDARD BIBLE, copyright 1960, 1962, 1963, 1968, 1971, 1972, 1973, 1975, 1977, 1995 by the Lockman Foundation. Used with permission.

A BRAND NEW JOURNEY WITH GOD

And they said to one another, "Were not our hearts burning within us while He was speaking to us on the road, while He was explaining the scriptures to us?" And they arose that very hour and returned to Jerusalem and found gathered together the eleven and those who were with them, saying, "The Lord has really risen and has appeared to Simon." And they began to relate their experience on the road and how He was recognized by them in the breaking of the bread.
Luke 24: 32-35

There is power in the Word. In this passage, their hearts burned within them because that's what the living word of God can do. The Bible says that 'God's word is living and active and sharper than a two edged sword'. Here is the real kicker, however. When revelation comes – when the word of God changes your life forever and you feel it burning within you - there is often a change of plans, too.

Notice what Cleopas and his friends did. They arose *that very hour!* They embarked on another journey - immediately.

Think about that for a minute. They had just arrived at their destination. They'd walked seven miles to get to Emmaus and were probably tired. It was late by this time. We know this because they urged Jesus to stay with them because of the lateness of the day. Yet *that very hour* they went back to Jerusalem to report to the disciples and other believers. A seven mile journey at night was probably a dangerous prospect, but the news was so important it couldn't wait. Their testimony was added to that of the other believers who had seen the Lord – an important story since it made it into scripture for us to read 2000 years later.

Cleopas and his friend started on a seven mile walk along a dusty road. I can only imagine that they were not in the best of spirits. After all, they'd just come from the most devastating event of their lives. But God had other plans. And it changed their lives forever.

Excerpted from *LIFE IS A HIGHWAY – Advice and Reflections On Navigating the Road of Life*. Copyright Tracy Krauss 2013.

Scripture references from the NEW AMERICAN STANDARD BIBLE, copyright 1960, 1962, 1963, 1968, 1971, 1972, 1973, 1975, 1977, 1995 by the Lockman Foundation. Used with permission.

LISTEN AND THEN GO

But an angel of the Lord spoke to Phillip saying, "Arise and go south to the road that descends from Jerusalem to Gaza." (This is the desert road) And he arose and went; and behold, there was an Ethiopian eunuch, a court official of Candace, queen of the Ethiopians, who was in charge of all her treasure; and he had come to Jerusalem to worship. And he was returning and sitting in his chariot and was reading the prophet Isaiah. And the Spirit said to Phillip, "Go up and join his chariot."
Acts 8: 26 - 29

If you know the rest of the story, you'll remember that the Ethiopian man gets saved and immediately is baptized by Phillip. What I love about this story is that right from the start, Phillip goes where God asks him to go – without question. Earlier in the story we find out that everyone else was going back to Jerusalem, (v 25) but Phillip goes a different way because God told him to. Next, notice how the timing was absolutely perfect. Any sooner or later, and Phillip would never have run into this Ethiopian traveller. But Phillip met the Ethiopian man right at the exact moment he was needed.

We never know when God will be calling us to do something, so be ready. It's a philosophy I use in my capacity as a writer. I have no idea who may pick up one of my books and be touched by something I've written. I've been privileged to hear feedback from readers expressing gratitude when a certain element of one of my stories impacted them. Similarly, I've had former students come back and tell me how I influenced their lives in a positive way. However, we won't always know the outcome of every deed we've done or word we've spoken. We may never know all the people we have influenced in this life, be it for harm or for good, but rest assured, God knows.

Excerpted from *LIFE IS A HIGHWAY – Advice and Reflections On Navigating the Road of Life*. Copyright Tracy Krauss 2013.

HE DIDN'T MAKE A MISTAKE

*For Thou did form my inward parts; Thou did weave me in
my mother's womb. I will give thanks to Thee for I am
fearfully and wonderfully made; wonderful are Thy works
and my soul knows it very well. My frame was not hidden
from Thee when I was made in secret and skillfully wrought
in the depths of the earth. Thine eyes have seen my unformed
being and in Thy book they were all written;
the days that were ordained for me
– when as yet there was not one of them...*
PSALMS 139: v 13 – 16

Each and every one of us is unique – a combination of
genetics and life experiences that will never be duplicated,
much like a snowflake.

I come from a long line of teachers – four generations to
be exact – as well as generally 'artsy' people. My grandmother
could quote long passages from Shakespeare, Longfellow and
Robbie Burns, which inspired my love of literature. My mother
was an eccentric artist known for painting on just about
anything, which undoubtedly influenced my passion for art. I
understand that my creative bent – perhaps even my
quirkiness - runs pretty deep. Even though I've always known
this, I didn't always accept it.

As a child all I wanted to do was draw. I literally filled
sketchbook after sketchbook. I was good at art, I loved to sing
and played several instruments, I was involved in drama, and I
had good grades. However, my athletic gene was pretty much
nonexistent. Every time we would have to pick teams in P.E.
class, I would wait with bated breath, hoping upon hope that I
wouldn't be picked last. For those who have ever gone through
this experience, you know that it hurts. Unfortunately, that is
often how it is in school – sports rule. For those of us that
aren't so inclined, P.E. can be your worst nightmare.

It's easy to still feel like that kid sometimes - inadequate
because you can't do something as well as someone else. Or
maybe what you are good at isn't valued in society as highly as
other things. It is important to recognize your uniqueness and

quit trying to fit into someone else's mold. God made you exactly the way He wanted you, quirks and all. It was a liberating experience when I finally fully embraced this truth. Jeremiah 1:5 says it well: *"Before I formed you in the womb I knew you; and before you were born I consecrated you..."*

Be the person God created you to be. Get to know yourself, then accept yourself, nurture yourself, and most importantly, love yourself. God does. So much so that he made you to be exactly the person he wanted.

Excerpted from *LIFE IS A HIGHWAY – Advice and Reflections On Navigating the Road of Life*. Copyright Tracy Krauss 2013.

Scripture references from the NEW AMERICAN STANDARD BIBLE, copyright 1960, 1962, 1963, 1968, 1971, 1972, 1973, 1975, 1977, 1995 by the Lockman Foundation. Used with permission.

Clinging to the Rock
MARCIA LEE LAYCOCK

A Small Patch of Blue

The day had been grey and dreary from beginning to end, a fine drizzle of rain falling continually, creating a thickening mist that shifted and swallowed all in its path. The next morning we were to drive to the high point on The Dome behind Dawson City, Yukon, and I prayed the morning sun would banish the fog and let us see the stunning view of the Klondike Valley. I hadn't seen it for many years and I longed for the exhilaration it had always given me.

But the next morning was not sunny. The fog lingered.

"Let's go up anyway," my husband said, "at least as far as the cemetery."

I knew what he intended. The cemetery held the graves of two good friends, men in their twenties who had taken their own lives in a suicide pact many years before. Their deaths had been the catalyst to the beginning of the journey that led us to faith in Jesus.

We parked the car at the gate and wandered among the graves, noting some names we recognized from years gone by, noting how young some of them had been when death claimed their mortal bodies.

We found the graves we were looking for – one marked by the idler wheel of a D6 Cat, the other by the front frame of another piece of heavy machinery. I watched quietly as my husband pushed scrub brush away so we could see their names welded on the unusual headstones. Memories of that time brought a quietness to both of us, and to the place.

Neither of us wanted to head back to town so we continued up the dirt road as it wound its way to the top. The peak of the Dome was above the clouds so we looked down on the grey shifting mist, watching as it slowly began to dissipate. A small patch of blue appeared. Part of the Yukon River. I was puzzled at first when I saw it emerge. At this point in the river's course, the Yukon is not blue. It's a milky grey, filled with the silt from a river upstream. Then I looked up and realized the river was reflecting the blue sky above it, slowly being revealed as the clouds moved away.

I thought of all the people who had come into our lives at that time of death and tragedy, people who prayed with us and guided us toward the truth about life, death and eternity. And I smiled. They themselves were just ordinary people, living ordinary lives in an isolated place, but they were reflecting something from beyond themselves. Something that glowed with the colour of vibrancy and life – the face of God.

I pray that will be the case with my life, with everything I do, everything I write. Though it may have little that is called extraordinary in its pages, though it may exist in a world filled with shifting fog, may it be a reflection of truth, flowing with the colour of true life, able to translate into healing, able to reflect the love of a holy God. May it draw my friends and readers along, as that small patch of blue river below us did, to a place where they will meet Him and know Him, just a little bit more than they did before.

"And as we have borne the image of the man of dust, we shall also bear the image of the heavenly Man" (1Cor.15:49).

ALMOST

"Tell me your story," my friend said.

I smiled and warned her that we might be there for a while, but she said she wanted to hear all of it. And I was excited because I love telling it, not because it's my story but because it is, from beginning to end, God's story. It becomes obvious to those listening and even more, to myself, that God's hand of protection has been over all of my life. There were so many times when I could have/should have had disastrous things happen; times when I almost died.

As my husband has said, "You walked into the fire and right out of it again with hardly a scratch!" Well, the smell of smoke often lingered, but he's right. I can relate to Shadrach, Meshach and Abednego.

There was that day I should have drowned but was saved, that night I could have been raped and even murdered but was left alone, that time I ingested a poison but it left no effect, the times I trusted strangers who could have been demons but turned out to be angels. Over and over again God protected me.

Oh yes, I have had my share of tragedies and trials, but even in those circumstances, God was there. There was the moment when I heard those mind-numbing words, you have cancer, the days when the chemo treatments were almost too much and others when I almost could not make myself walk through the doors of the clinic where I would lay on a table and allow radiation to burn my body. There was that day I was almost overcome when I realized the child I carried would not be born alive and the day I got the phone call telling me my father had died. There were those years when the pain of the circumstances almost drove me to curse God.

In all of those times it was God's presence, and above all His love, that kept me sane, kept me going, and kept me in the shelter of his wings. It was Jesus who kept me from going beyond 'almost.'

I love that old song that says, "The Name of the Lord is a strong tower, the righteous run into it and they are safe." The words are true. The name Jesus keeps us safe, even in the midst of the fire or in the midst of a raging storm – not always safe from pain, but safe from separation from Him. And that is the only agony we would not survive.

These words are also true: "But we have this treasure in jars of clay to show that this all-surpassing power is from God and not from us. We are hard pressed on every side, but not crushed; perplexed but not in despair, persecuted but not abandoned; struck down but not destroyed" (2Corinthians 4:7-9).

That is our testimony, our story as believers in Christ Jesus. When we have Him we will always have that word, almost.

CLINGING TO THE ROCK

The far north is a place where things are pared down, taken to the lowest common denominators of life: rock, water, sun, insects and wind. And of course, in the winter, the world is pared down even more, to the denominators of snow and ice. It is a place where the word survival is never far from one's thoughts.

So it was a marvel to me how the tiny delicate flowers of Baffin Island could survive. There is very little soil yet they spring up and cling to solid rock. Vibrant dwarf fireweed, saxifrage, anemones and the ever-present Arctic cotton abound. The tundra seemed to be in motion as they swayed in the constant wind, lifting their heads toward a far-away sun. We stepped around them, our heads bent in homage, our camera shutters clicking.

As I moved across that barren landscape I couldn't help but think of the barren landscape of cancer I have been wandering in. The similarities are stark. There isn't much to hang onto at times. The winds of fear and loss seem always in my face and the sun can seem oh so far away. But I stared at a bright yellow anemone and took heart. If this little one can survive in this, her desolate place, then so shall I in mine, by doing what she does season after season. Cling to the rock.

There are times in everyone's life, in every writer's life when this is necessary. We tend to think of these times in a negative way. As when we envision a harsh northern climate, we hear the word, cancer, and shudder. Yet there are those wildflowers. There are moments when God's presence is so real the beauty of his grace is all that matters. There are those times when you know He's carrying you across this barren landscape.

Our Rock is more solid and everlasting than those slowly disintegrating across the tundra. Our Rock speaks and comforts and holds our hand. Our Rock carries us when our knees buckle and cradles our head when we just need to cry. Our Rock hides us in his cleft and sets our feet on a firm foundation.

And when I "lift up my eyes to the hills," and ask, "Where does my help come from?" He answers - "My help comes from the Lord, Maker of heaven and earth. He will not let your foot slip, he who watches over you will not slumber ... The Lord watches over you, the Lord is your shade at your right hand; the sun will not harm you by day nor the moon by night. The Lord will keep you from all harm, he will watch over your life;

the Lord will watch over your coming going both now and forevermore" (Psalm 121:1-8).

If you are in a barren place in your life, medically, physically, emotionally or spiritually, take heart. You can be like those Arctic flowers - cling to the Rock.

CONSIDERING TIME

"Did having cancer alter your perspective on time?"

My friend waited while I thought about her question.

"I'm sure it has," I finally responded, "but I'm not quite sure how."

Her question got me thinking and as I thought about it, I was surprised to realize that I no longer look at time as rushing by. I no longer get a panicky feeling when I think of all the things I want to accomplish in my day, my week, my life. I am much more inclined to take the time to stop and consciously make myself aware of what's happening around me.

That surprised me. I would have thought I'd feel more pressure, knowing that life is short and can end at any time (waking up on a respirator in ICU makes you keenly aware of that fact). But, since having cancer, I'm not so focused on the urgency to do as the desire to be. I stepped out onto a windy winter street this morning and delighted in the falling snow and stood for a moment to watch the swirl of brown leaves kissing the gleaming windows of tall buildings. The urgency to get my Christmas shopping done fell away and time seemed to settle as softly as the falling snow.

It's easy to get caught up in the "tyranny of the urgent," especially as we creep closer to the age when death is peeping around the corner. It's easy to get that panicky feeling in our stomachs as we approach the end of the year and know it's time to make plans for another. But it's also easy, I've discovered, to "be still and know" that He is God and that with His hand in ours fear and even the pounding pulse of time, melts away.

My husband is known for quoting John Piper who said that at the root of all sin is unbelief. I realized as I stood on that street the other day that my panicky feelings were just that, lack of faith in God. Knowing that I was seconds away from meeting Him face to face has restored that faith, given me peace, and yes, changed my perspective on time.

Time is no longer a task-master but simply the measure of the journey we are all taking, one that will lead to that face to face meeting with our Heavenly Father. I know I won't escape it and neither will you. I look forward to it, knowing it is not an end but a new beginning.

I will still sit down in early 2013 to make my list of goals and challenges for the New Year, but this time it will be with a smile on my face, not a frown, knowing that time may stop at any moment and that new beginning will be a shining reality.

Go to Your Altars

At a recent writing seminar those attending were challenged to write the last few words we would give to the world before we died. A sobering thought. I'd been thinking a lot about altars lately, since I had been doing a Bible study on the ancient tabernacle and how it relates to us today. The study led us to realize that we are now the temple, the place where the Spirit of God resides on this earth. Another sobering thought.

The Bible study detailed the role of the various altars and furniture used in the tabernacle that was built and carried by the Hebrew people during their time in the wilderness. They were instructed in the construction and placement of the altar of sacrifice, the altar of incense, the table of the bread, the lamp stand and the brazen laver and, most significant of all, the ark of the covenant that sat behind the veil in the Holy of Holies. Each one had a specific purpose. At each altar the priests were to perform specific rites for the atonement of the sins of the nation.

That led me to wonder – if I am a temple, where are my altars? Do I have an altar of sacrifice - that place where I lay down that which is precious to me as an offering to the Lord? I should do so daily, within the sincerity of my heart. Do I have a brazen laver where I wash myself before entering God's presence? I should do so on my knees, humbled to know that I can proceed into His presence because of the spilling of His Son's blood that has washed my sins away forever. Do I have an altar of incense, that place from which praise and prayer and worship emanate? Again, it should be a daily practice, erupting from my mind and my mouth like a fountain.

Do I have a table, where the bread, the body of my Lord, is displayed in all its simplicity and glory? Is there a lamp stand, that place that burns with His holy fire that can never be extinguished? I must hold it up high for all to see. And is there an ark in me, a place where the remembrances of God's faithfulness and holiness are kept? I should cherish them in the depths of my soul, bowing before that mercy seat and acknowledging the forgiveness He has extended to me by His death on that cross.

These altars all require my service, the death of my own agendas and ambitions, the breaking of my pride and a bowing down to His sovereignty.

So these are my few words, words that I would say to myself and to all of us who would be believers in Christ –

Go to Your Altars: the altar of incense, shouting out praise, petitions and songs; the altar of washing, bathing in His mercy, acknowledging His grace; the altar of the lamp stand, feeding the flame of faith as a light to the world; the altar of sacrifice, relinquishing your ambitions, your dreams and your pride.

Go to your altars. Lay yourself down.

HARD QUESTIONS

It seemed fitting that the sky hung heavy and low. It seemed right that the wind was bitter, howling with the fierce shriek of winter around a tiny country cemetery. There was a very small hole in the ground and a very tiny casket to be put into it. It seemed appropriate that we all stood numbed by the cold of that day.

A friend of mine once wrote a poem about Adam, Eve and God in the Garden of Eden. It was a good poem, well constructed with a strong rhythm and powerful images. One of those images often comes to mind when bad things happen to good people. It's an image of God curled into a fetal position, and the wailing sound of His weeping.

Sometimes we ask hard questions. Why did that baby have to die, God? Why is my friend suffering with a painful cancer? Why are those people in Africa starving? We don't usually get a good answer to those questions. They leave us numb and they leave us wondering if God is there.

But then there is that image and that sound. In my friend's poem God mourned the first disobedience, the first break in His relationship with the creatures He put on the earth. The picture my friend painted with his words was of a God who cares, a God who feels our pain, a God who mourns with us, especially at the graves of tiny babies.

He is also a God who will answer. He is a God who acted to redeem all that was broken in our world. He is a God who continues to do so. The redemption was accomplished on the cross of Calvary, but it is not yet complete. As the writer of the book of Hebrews said, God "... waits for his enemies to be made his footstool, because by one sacrifice he has made perfect forever those who are being made holy" (Hebrews 10:13).

The process is sometimes painful, but the world will one day be made entirely new, entirely redeemed. The scriptures talk about creation groaning as we wait for that day. The groans do not fall on deaf ears, nor will they remain unanswered forever. One day that tiny baby will rise, whole and perfect as God intended him to be.

God's plan is unfolding. What then, should we do in those times when we groan and feel there is no answer? Again, scripture tells us – "And what does the Lord require of you? To act justly, to love mercy and to walk humbly with your God" (Micah 6:8).

Humility before God bows the knee and continues to believe. Humility before God acknowledges His sovereignty and calls Him good. Even when babies die and the pain of this world overwhelms, humility before God says, "Blessed be the name of the Lord."

JUST LIKE HIM

My eyes fluttered open to the sound of howling wind. More snow, I thought, and thought about slipping deeper under the covers. But I was awake so I headed to the kitchen to make my usual cup of coffee and start the day. I expected there would be another few inches of snow on our deck and the thought didn't make me happy. Coffee in hand, I wandered to our back door. Yes, there was another thick layer of the white stuff, but there was something else that caught my eye. Something unusual - a smiley face, grinning at me. There, on the side of our barbecue's cover was a perfect smiley, eyes and all.

It made me laugh out loud. And then tears came to my eyes. You see, I'd been feeling a little blue lately, a little "under the weather," as the saying goes. I've been chalking it up to the grey days we've been having lately, combined with the fact that I've had some health issues that haven't been fun to deal with over the past while. I tried to talk myself out of the 'funk' by reminding myself of all that I have to be thankful for. That helped, but the grey mood still lingered. So I asked the Lord to lighten my spirits a little.

He knew just how to do it.

As I stood there grinning back at our barbecue, I thought of all the other times He has done something similar. The time he made a tiny flower glow with the promise of hope in my living room as I lay on our couch aching from chemo treatments; the day he showed me a perfect rosebud that had just bloomed in a Papua New Guinea garden when I was struggling to walk after being hit by a debilitating virus; the day he showed me the delight in my three-year-old nephew's eyes when he saw a cluster of blue irises for the first time; the morning my mom woke my brother and I so we could see the marmot that had taken up residence in a pile of logs beside our house. These were all 'smiley' moments – moments of delight sent by the hand of God. It's just like Him to know exactly what we need at exactly the perfect time.

We shouldn't be surprised. The scripture tells us He delights in delighting us. "For the Lord takes delight in his people; he crowns the humble with victory" (Psalm 149:4).

The Scripture also says "because of the Lord's great love we are not consumed, for his compassions never fail. They are new every morning; great is your faithfulness" (Lam.3:22,23).

And "great are the works of the Lord; they are pondered by all who delight in them" (Psalm 111:2).

Are you a bit "under the weather" these days? Ponder the works, the love, the faithfulness of our Lord. And don't be afraid to ask him to lighten your spirit. It's just like Him to find the perfect way to do it.

A LOST OPPORTUNITY

It must have looked like this was an important prisoner. He was guarded by two hundred soldiers, seventy horsemen and two hundred spearmen. They had heard there were men who wanted him dead, so they had taken measures to ensure his safety. He was, after all, a Roman citizen. When they arrived without incident at their destination, the man was handed over to the Roman governor of the province. His trial lasted only long enough for two witnesses to make their statements and for the prisoner himself to plead his innocence. There really was not enough evidence to imprison the man, but the governor, the "most excellent Felix" (Acts 24:3), put the prisoner, the apostle Paul, under house arrest.

From time to time Felix would have Paul brought before him and the apostle would tell him about "righteousness, self-control and the judgment to come" (Acts 24:25). Many times he talked with Felix about faith in Jesus Christ. Felix heard Paul's story, listened to his discourse. At times he was afraid and sent him away. But he kept calling him back. He kept calling him back over a period of two years!

As I read this story in the book of Acts, I wondered about the battle that must have been going on in that Roman governor's mind and soul. He heard the words of truth, but, sadly, there was something else of more importance to him. Verse 26 says – "At the same time he was hoping that Paul would offer him a bribe, so he sent for him frequently and talked with him."

Felix was so focused on what he wanted that he missed what he really needed. His greed blinded him to the most costly gift God could offer, and though it was offered for free, he did not receive it. Then he was replaced as governor and the opportunity, as far as we know, was lost.

I wonder how often we do the same. We too are sometimes so focused on our wants that we miss the one thing we really need – a growing relationship with Jesus Christ. The pursuit of prosperity and happiness too often supersedes the pursuit of our spiritual well-being. We should all heed Paul's words, those he no doubt spoke to Felix as he did to the people in a place called Corinth – "I tell you, now is the time of God's favor, now is the day of salvation" (2 Corinthians 6:2b).

Opportunities to receive God's gifts are offered to us every day. Grace, forgiveness and righteousness are available for free. They were purchased for us by the Son of God. All we have to do is receive them.

ORDINARILY

Ordinarily I don't like it when people send me those forwarded-forwarded-forwarded emails. Ordinarily I consider them a waste of time and often delete them without opening them. But lately a dear friend who knows what it's like to be facing an illness like cancer has been sending them regularly. She has picked beautiful pictures, inspirational thoughts and, best of all, laugh-out-loud jokes. I've been reading them and I must admit I've even gotten to the point where I look forward to finding one in my inbox each day.

I guess my idea of wasted time has shifted a bit. I stare out the front window of our home more often, just to watch the wind ripple on the pond across the street - (I call it pondering ;0). Each time I walk by them I lean down to smell the flowers my husband bought me last week when I had to spend the day having tests at the hospital. I scratch my cat's ears more than I used to. I stand on our back deck, watch the clouds and listen to the laughter of our neighbor's children. I lay awake in the morning and stare at the outline of my husband's face in the early morning sun. The accumulation of these little things seems to make a difference as life has slowed into a rhythm of waiting.

I've also found that scriptures - those oh-so- familiar passages that can seem trite or even cliché at times - have a whole new depth now that I have a deeper understanding of my need for them. I get regular emails with scripture delivered to my inbox too, and I open them first. The accumulation of verses seems to make a difference when my mood slips a little, when my heart is longing for something beyond this reality to hang onto.

One of the passages that arrived recently was this one from Philippians 4:8 -"whatever is true, whatever is noble, whatever is right, whatever is pure, whatever is lovely, whatever is admirable ... if anything is excellent or praiseworthy... think about such things."

I noticed there was no action connected to this passage, just thinking. You can do that anytime, anywhere, but to do it deeply you have to slow down a little. You have to pause, perhaps stare out a window at a small pond, and just think.

Ordinarily I wouldn't be doing such things. My life would be bustling with urgencies like deadlines and projects and to-do lists. But there is nothing ordinary about living with cancer. It changes things. It changes you. Ordinarily I would think that a bad thing but now I treasure it. I treasure the tingling awareness of this world now that I know how tenuous my hold on it really is. I treasure the small things, the pondering.

Interesting - I seem to be smiling a lot.

IS IT REALLY HOPE?

I recently read a hilarious book by Terry Pratchett called Going Postal. If you're a fan of fantasy, you're probably aware of this prolific writer. His imagined worlds are intriguing, his characters quirky, his plots ingenious. I thoroughly enjoyed Going Postal - often laughing out loud as I read it.

But it had one flaw. The main character, Moist Von Lipwig (that's Lip-vig, if you please!), is a con man. He lives his life by one belief - people will always have hope, and if you're smart enough, you can figure a way to make them pay you for it.

The problem is Mr. Lipwig's definition of the word hope is flawed. To him, the reality of hope means he can make you believe the piece of glass he holds in his hand is really a priceless diamond that he will sell you for a ridiculously low price. He knows that part of you will know that "diamond" is not real, but part of you is thinking, what if? Part of you wants to believe what he's telling you. Mr. Lipwig becomes skilled at convincing people that his lies will make them rich. Mr. Lipvig plays not on hope, but on greed.

True hope is something very different indeed. The writer of the book of Romans explains – "Not only so, but we ourselves who have the first fruits of the Spirit groan inwardly as we wait eagerly for our adoption as sons, the redemption of our bodies. For in this hope we were saved. But hope that is seen is no hope at all. Who hopes for what he already has? But if we hope for what we do not yet have, we wait for it patiently" (Romans 8:23-25).

Pratchett is using the dictionary definition of the word – "expectation and desire combined."(Canadian Oxford Dictionary). Not a bad definition, but in Prachett's story we would have to add the greed ingredient – the lust for those things we see in the world around us. To bring us back to the word hope, I would add the biblical addendum – "hope that is seen is no hope at all."

Scripture tells us that the whole of creation groans with the anticipation of being redeemed and reunited with the creator. That's the hope we have, the hope that makes us long for the intimacy of relationship with God, the hope that keeps us hanging on when things look dark, the hope that tells us there is something more than we can see.

"I pray ... that the eyes of your heart may be enlightened in order that you may know the hope to which he has called you, the riches of his glorious inheritance in the saints, and his incomparably great power for us who believe. That power is like the working of his mighty strength, which he exerted in Christ when he raised him from the dead and seated him at his right hand in the heavenly realms, far above all rule and authority, power and dominion, and every title that can be given, not only in the present age but also in the one to come" (Ephesians 1:18-21).

WHEN GOD PUTS YOU IN THE SIDECAR

My husband is a motorcycle enthusiast. So far he hasn't gone out and bought one, but whenever he sees one he likes on the road he'll point it out and say, "Nice bike," then look at me to gauge my reaction. We were sitting at a stoplight not long ago and a shiny motorcycle pulled up beside us. It had a sidecar attached.

"There we go," Spence said.

I laughed, imagining what it would be like to ride in such a little appendage. "I think I'd rather be on the bike with you," I said, "or better yet, on one of my own." Sidecars are for kids, I thought. You don't have any control in a sidecar; you just have to hang on and try to enjoy the ride.

It seems God has put me in a sidecar for a time. I've just been diagnosed with cancer and suddenly my life is not mine to control. Doctors are telling me what will happen, when and where I will go. I don't really want to experience any of what they're telling me I will go through. But I have no choice. All I can do is hang on and find ways to cope with the ride.

In the book of John, Jesus tells the apostle Peter about a time when the same thing would happen to him. "I tell you the truth, when you were younger you dressed yourself and went where you wanted; but when you are old you will stretch out your hands and someone else will dress you and lead you where you do not want to go." Jesus said this to indicate the kind of death by which Peter would glorify God. Then he said to him, "Follow me!" (John 21:18-19)

I don't know exactly what lies ahead for me. I'm hopeful that this cancer can be eradicated and I'll go on with my life. I'm praying my time in the sidecar will be short. But perhaps God has another plan. In the meantime, I take encouragement from those few words, "by which Peter would glorify God." What happened to him was not in vain. It had a purpose. The events of our lives all have purpose and are meant to bring glory to God. We have agency in that, by his grace and mercy, and that fruit will be a blessing not just to others but to us as we journey down that road.

I'm spurred on too, by the next words Jesus spoke. "Follow me!" That's a path Peter tried hard to take, one that changed him into a man of God, a leader of men. It's a path that leads to "a spacious place," (Ps. 18:19), where God's presence is evident, to the joy that comes in understanding God's undying love and the peace that makes us lean into the wind and relish every moment on this earth – even moments in the sidecar.

"but the Lord was my support. He brought me out into a spacious place; he rescued me because he delighted in me" (Psalm 18:18-19).

TENSION

I love books with a lot of tension on the page - books that make you grip them a little harder than others, books that make you hold your breath.

I love the Bible for that very reason. There are so many stories in it that do all of the above. The story of Joseph, for instance, especially the scene where his brothers come before him in Egypt to beg for food, not knowing this man is the brother they betrayed. The tension on that page is palpable. What will Joseph do? Has he forgiven them or will he punish them and get his revenge at last? And the tension is drawn out as he plays games with them, throws them in jail, tells them to leave and come back again, tells them not to return without their youngest brother. (A lot of lessons for a writer to learn here). Through it all we wonder what God is doing, how this drama will play out and how God will be glorified. Even when we know the end of the story, it makes us hold our breath.

My husband preached on this passage a while ago, and talked a bit about the tension - this is a short excerpt -

"The disguise of grace promises that one day there will be a great reveal. It's what makes the tension grow in this story, the anticipation of what it will be like when the brothers finally know who he is, when the father is finally reunited with the son that was lost. All these are prompts to us of an even greater day of revealing. Every act of disguised grace here below has the purpose in it of knowing the author of this grace for who He really is, of being brought close to the Father. The Great Reveal is coming soon."

There has been a great deal of tension in the world lately, a great deal of drama. Many who are watching are grasping onto material things a little harder, hoping they won't slip away. Many are holding their breath as they wonder what's going to happen.

But, like the story of Joseph and many others in the Bible, we know what's in the last chapter. We know God's grace and mercy will be revealed. We know He will be glorified, whatever happens. Because, as my husband said - "He who lived His life mostly in a disguise of grace, was revealed through the resurrection as the King of Kings and Lord of Lords."

Psalm 33 says it so well - "Let all the earth fear the Lord; let all the people of the world revere Him. For he spoke and it came to be; he commanded and it stood firm. The Lord foils the plans of the nations; he thwarts the purposes of the peoples. But the plans of the Lord stand firm forever, the purposes of his heart through all generations. Blessed is the nation whose God is the Lord, the people he chose for his inheritance. From heaven the Lord looks down and sees all mankind; from his dwelling place he watches all who live on earth - he who forms the hearts of all, who considers everything they do. No king is saved by the size of his army; no warrior escapes by his great strength. A horse is a vain hope for deliverance; despite all its great strength it cannot save. But the eyes of the Lord are on those who fear him, on those whose hope is in his unfailing love, to deliver them from death and keep them alive in famine. We wait in hope for the Lord; he is our help and our shield. In him our hearts rejoice, for we trust in his holy name. May your unfailing love rest upon us, O Lord, even as we put our hope in you." (Psalm 33:8-22).

Moments in the Word

JANICE L. DICK

BANQUETS OF INSIGNIFICANCE

When Jesus looked up and saw a great crowd coming toward
him, he said to Philip,
"Where shall we buy bread for these people to eat?"
Philip answered him, "It would take more than half a year's
wages to buy enough bread for each one to have a bite!"
Another of his disciples, Andrew, Simon Peter's brother,
spoke up, "Here is a boy with five small barley loaves and
two small fish, but how far will they go among so many?"
John 6:5-9 NIV

REFLECTION:

In this world of exponentially increasing knowledge, we may often feel that our meager contribution is insignificant. A few volunteer hours will not change a political decision. A meal for a neighbor will not alter a difficult life situation. A prayer and a hug will not fix a broken heart. What can we offer that would make a significant difference to anyone, or that hasn't already been said or done? This self-doubt is based on the premise that small acts are inconsequential. According to John 6, this is a false premise.

Five thousand hungry people are waiting for a real meal deal, and there are no fast food restaurants in sight. In the midst of the dilemma, Jesus asks the disciples for their input. Apparently, he wants them to come up with a solution.

Focus first on Phillip. His response is practical. "There is no way we can possibly feed this crowd, not even if we had a ton of cash on us, which we don't." If I'm honest, this sounds like something I might have said. "What do you expect of us? We don't have the ability or the resources to handle this. You can test our faith, but we must face the facts."

While Phillip and I are voicing our excuses, another disciple quietly approaches Jesus. We almost miss him. He has something in his hands. "Umm, I know it's not much, Master, but I've found some bread and a coupla fish." Without further comment, he hands them to Jesus and steps back expectantly. He's done what he could with what he had, not realizing he's just contributed to a miracle.

Do you see the difference between the Phillip and Andrew in this portion of Scripture? They've both been with Jesus, but Andrew has been observing, learning, growing. His faith had deepened as he's watched Jesus deal with other impossible situations. He has been considering the power of the Master. So, he gathers up what is insignificant to anyone else and offers it to the Lord. Jesus uses his offering, and Andrew's faith is catapulted to the next level. He realizes the Master is not limited as he himself is, and thousands are blessed.

I find great encouragement in this Scripture passage to do my best with what I've been given. After all, it is the Lord who hands out our gifts and talents, and He expects us to use them.

PRAYER:

Lord, may we not neglect to offer our meager lunch to you.

Perhaps you will choose to make a banquet of it.

AN ANALOGY OF SALVATION

"If he has done you any wrong or owes you anything, charge it to me."

Philemon 18 NIV

REFLECTION:

Philemon, the man to whom this brief New Testament letter is addressed, lived in Colossae, an Asian city 130 miles from the Aegean Sea in what is now southwest Turkey. He was a Christian, but in that society, slave ownership was normal. Philemon had a slave named Onesimus, whose name meant "useful," but until this time, Onesimus had not been useful to his master. He had stolen from him then run away, crimes that were punishable by death.

The circumstance that changed Onesimus' life was his meeting with the Apostle Paul, and through him, with Jesus Christ. He was divinely forgiven for his crimes and received full status as a follower of Christ. Paul had grown to love this young slave, but there was still the problem of settling things with Philemon. After all, the slave had wronged his master.

Paul took things into his own hands and launched an appeal to Philemon, with whom he was also familiar, asking him to accept his errant slave as a brother in Christ and to forgive him for his thievery. In his appeal to Philemon, Paul organized his words after the manner of the ancient Greek and Roman teachers: build rapport, persuade the mind, move the emotions. He called on Philemon's sense of fairness, reminding him that he actually owed Paul his very life, but that if restitution were required, Paul would pay it. His strong appeal cannot have been lost on Philemon.

Look for a moment at the bones of this account: We have one righteous, who is Philemon. He has been wronged and restitution must be made. We have one guilty, who is Onesimus. He cannot undo what he has done and stands sentenced to death. Enter Paul, seeking to make things right between them, to restore their relationship, even improve it markedly. As mediator, he understands both sides, but he goes a huge step further by announcing that he himself will accept the charges for the guilty one.

Recognize the analogy? God is righteous; we are guilty. Christ steps in to reconnect us, even though the only way is for Him to accept our punishment of death. That accomplished, we are lifted to acceptance with God the Father.

How thankful we can be that we have One who stands in the gap for us so we can be made right in the sight of God. What the analogy fails to show, however, is that in our case, it was God the Father who initiated the plan for our salvation before the beginning of time. Indeed, there can be no greater love.

PRAYER:
Dear Father God, we bow in humble acceptance of Your divine plan. We praise You for seeking us out, for sending Jesus to take our punishment so that we could be right with You, for giving us Your Dear Spirit to comfort and guide us.

LOOKING BUSY

"But about that day or hour no one knows, not even the
angels in heaven, nor the Son, but only the Father. Be on
guard! Be alert! You do not know when that time will come."
Mark 13:32,33 NIV

REFLECTION:

Recently, I heard a comedian on the radio attempting to make light of Christianity. He painted a verbal picture of people walking about wearing cardboard signs announcing, "Jesus is coming." After several sarcastic comments he said, "So if Jesus really is coming, at least look busy!"

His comments were not particularly funny to me, but they did carry a valid message. You see, I believe with all my heart that Jesus is coming, although I don't know when. As Mark states in chapter 13:32, *"No one knows the day or the hour."* Does my life show that I believe in the imminent return of Christ or do I waste my time with relatively unimportant matters? Do my relationships and actions portray a sense of urgency because the time is short or do I spend my time entertaining myself? Do I even look busy with regard to His soon return?

First of all, we don't want to just look busy, pretending to live according to the Word of God to look good or attract attention. There are many imposters, as there have been throughout the ages—John calls them "antichrists" in I John 2:18—but we don't want to be one of them. It is essential that we know Christ personally and live for him because we love him and have chosen to follow his call in our lives.

Secondly, we need to *be* busy, putting out the word that Christ is seeking to save souls while there is time. In fact, he is already here, shining through us who represent his kingdom on earth as we mix and connect with our fellow humans. Our keeping busy may not involve marching in sandwich signs (please don't ask me to do that), but we should definitely be about the King's business.

That task will differ in each of our lives as we trust in and follow our Lord. We don't choose to be a spectacle for the sake of the shock factor or for unpleasant attention, but we can never forget that we are called, chosen, commanded by our Master to be about his will for us.

Whether our calling is to be a mechanic, a singer, a politician or a writer of books and articles, we must commit to do our best. Because we never know when our time will be up. The exact moment of Christ's return is a mystery to us, but the fact of his coming is sure. In response to that fact, we each have a job to do. Do we really need sarcastic comedians to encourage us to make the most of our time?

PRAYER:
Lord Jesus, let us focus on You and Your will for us, striving to do our best in whatever that is.

LIFE'S A ROLLERCOASTER

The people ate and were satisfied...the disciples picked up seven basketfuls of broken pieces that were left over....
The Pharisees came and began to question Jesus...
they asked him for a sign....
Then [Jesus] began to teach [the disciples] that the Son of Man must suffer many terrible things...He must be killed, and after three days rise again....
After six days Jesus took Peter, James and John with him and led them up a high mountain....There he was transfigured before them. His clothes became dazzling white...."
Mark 8:8-9,11, 31; 9:2-4 NIV

REFLECTION:
There are many ups and downs in our lives. Some days we feel on top of the world. The sun shines and joy infuses us even as we breathe. Then there are those other days we've all experienced when things go wrong from the moment we open our eyes and realize the alarm wasn't turned on, until we crawl into bed and remember that Junior needs a decorated birthday cake for Kindergarten tomorrow. Our joy seeps away and we feel as if we never had it.

Check out the rollercoaster of events and emotions from the preceding Scripture verses:

☺ Jesus feeds four thousand people—and there are leftovers

☹ Jesus is met by the local Jewish leaders who demand a miracle to prove his claims

☹ Jesus describes to His followers His imminent suffering and death

☺ Jesus takes Peter, James and John to the top of a mountain to see him transformed That already seems like enough of an emotional ride, in my opinion, but in the time it takes Jesus and his followers to descend the Mount of Transfiguration, their emotions are again assaulted by the blood-chilling shrieks of a demon-possessed boy. ☹ Without hesitation Jesus rebukes the demon and reaches out to touch the boy with healing hands. ☺ Heaven and hell again.

I'm sure the disciples must have wondered what had become of their lives and when things would return to normal. Wondered like you and I do when things go from bad to better to bad again. What is expected of us? Are we really on the right path?

According to Jesus' example, the proper response to life's rollercoaster is accepting our lot and doing what God asks us to do. That makes normal different for everyone because God's call to each of us is unique. That makes the situation I'm in right now, whatever it is, normal for me.

PRAYER:
Lord, next time I'm on a spiritual or emotional rollercoaster, help me to remember how you handled the ups and downs and do likewise.

"I've been a great deal happier since I have given up thinking about what is easy and pleasant, and being discontented because I couldn't have my own will. Our life is determined for us; and it makes the mind very free when we give up wishing, and only think of bearing what is laid upon us, and doing what is given us to do."
George Eliot

LIMITATIONS

*Now there is in Jerusalem near the Sheep Gate a pool, which
in Aramaic is called Bethesda....Here a great number of
disabled people used to lie. One who was there had been an
invalid for thirty-eight years. When Jesus saw him lying
there and learned that he had been in this condition for a long
time, he asked him, "Do you want to get well?"
"Sir," the invalid replied, "I have no one to help me into the
pool when the water is stirred. While I am trying to get in,
someone else goes down ahead of me."
Then Jesus said to him, "Get up! Pick up your mat and walk."
At once the man was cured; he picked up his mat and walked.*
John 5:2-9 NIV

REFLECTION:

We are all acquainted with the limitations placed upon us
by our humanity. In spite of new discoveries, inventions and
information bombarding us every day, we still fall prey to
illness and loss, and are bound by time and space. Even in this
age of technology and advanced medical science, we are not
free of limitations.

The paralyzed man spoken of in John 5 had never known
anything but limitations. He couldn't walk or work, so he was
constantly dependent on others for his most basic needs. It's
impossible to know what he felt like if we haven't been in his
situation, but I imagine he was often or always discouraged,
frustrated, overwhelmed. Eventually, his disability spread
from his body to his mind. He had tunnel vision as far as his
healing was concerned—when the angel stirred the water, he
had to be the first one in—and no one cared enough to help
him.

Except Jesus. But even as the Creator of the universe bent
over him, the man could not visualize healing, because he was
unable to look beyond what he understood. He didn't want to
talk; he wanted help to get into the pool. With characteristic
compassion, Jesus healed him in spite of his doubts and lack
of understanding.

How often do we respond to our Lord in like manner? "Thanks for Your concern, Lord, but nothing can be done," or, "You don't know what I'm facing right now." We forget who we're speaking to. He has sought us out to bless us, and he will, but sometimes he holds off as he awaits our trust. Do we believe that he is sincere? That he is able? That he will not necessarily use the prescribed or expected means of healing? His ways and knowledge are as far beyond ours as the heavens are above the earth, or as the east is from the west.

If we broaden our faith, and sometimes even if we don't, he tells us to pick up our respective mats and walk, because the power of our God has no limits.

PRAYER:

Dear Father, we praise you because you are so great, so powerful, so compassionate. We thank you for remembering that we are human, for accepting and forgiving us, for blessing us because you are love.

RECOGNITION

Now bands of raiders from Aram had gone out and had taken captive a young girl from Israel, and she served Naaman's wife. She said to her mistress, 'If only my master would see the prophet who is in Samaria! He would cure him of his leprosy.' Naaman went to his master and told him what the girl from Israel had said.
II Kings 5:2-4 NIV

REFLECTION:

I don't know about you, but I like to be recognized for what I do. Oh, I know we're not supposed to be that way, but if we are honest, our service often carries a price tag.

The heroine of II Kings 5 was an exception to the usual. Kidnapped from her home at a young age by Aramean raiders and forced into slavery, this Israelite girl could have been fearful, cowering, angry, bitter, or all of the above because of what she had endured and the life she'd been compelled to assume. She could have been shattered and useless to her mistress.

Instead, we see a child who obviously chose a positive, giving attitude over a defeated life, someone who chose to serve faithfully, cheerfully and with compassion the very people who had robbed her of everything familiar. This child had chosen to serve with no strings attached. She had learned the true meaning of service—a giving spirit.

Her master, Naaman, suffered from leprosy, "a serious disease that causes painful rough areas on the skin and that badly damages nerves and flesh" (http://www.merriam-webster.com/dictionary/leprosy). As the text states, the slave girl, prompted by a memory from her childhood, suggests to her mistress that there was a prophet of God in Israel who can heal Naaman. The message is relayed to him, he follows up on it, and is miraculously healed. He returns to Aram a new man, within and without (read the entire story in II Kings 5).

I would like to think that when Naaman of the Smooth Skin returned home, he asked for the girl and honored her by inviting her to eat at his table for the rest of her life, that he asked her to tell him about her God, that he granted her freedom for her gift of kindness. But Scripture does not tell us that. In fact, it never mentions the girl again. She earns no earthly recognition at all.

Would I be willing to continue to compassionately serve a man whose life I had indirectly saved, even if he never mentioned my contribution? As I go about my daily life, am I willing to keep my left hand from knowing what my right hand is doing, serving my Master for His sake and not my own recognition?

Jesus states, as recorded in Matthew 6:6, *"Then your Father, who sees what is done in secret, will reward you."* This truth was enough for the Israelite slave girl. Is it enough for me?

PRAYER:

"Lord, help me to leave recognition and rewards in Your hands and to serve You faithfully and compassionately all my days."

THE DANGER OF THE FAMILIAR

SCRIPTURE:
When they came to Jesus, they saw the man who had been possessed by the legion of demons,
sitting there, dressed and in his right mind; and they were afraid. . . Then the people began to beg Jesus to leave their region. (Read the entire story in Mark 5:1 - 20.)
Mark 5:15-17 NIV

REFLECTION:
The people in the region of the Gerasenes were familiar with the demoniac who lived among the tombs. They had tried many times to restrain him, without success. Even leg-irons couldn't hold him; the spirits within him were too strong. If people ventured near the tombs, they heard his unearthly screams ripping the air, and they shuddered. They hated the presence of the man there, but . . . they were familiar with him. He had become an unwelcome but accepted phenomenon.

The Gerasenes thought they wanted to be rid of the demon-possessed man, but when Jesus healed him and sent the demons into a herd of pigs that leapt to their deaths in the sea, the locals were more upset about the loss of bacon than the obviously changed man. They were used to hellish roarings at all hours of the day and night, but afraid of a man clothed and in his right mind. They didn't know him, didn't understand him, and so they were afraid. They were doubly afraid of the Man who had instigated the changes.

We tend to judge the Gerasenes. What were they thinking? The dangerous demoniac had been healed. They—and he—were safe from his torment. Peace and quiet had been restored. Why were they not pleased with these results?

Perhaps we judge too quickly. How often do we respond in the same way, afraid of the unfamiliar? When Jesus walks into our world and begins to order it aright, how often do we hide behind familiarity and cling to the common? How often do we obstruct the work of the Spirit because we fear His renovation in our lives?

Renovation makes a mess before it improves things. Often we deny our Lord the opportunity to transform us because we would rather not deal with the mess, the pigs plunging into the lake.

Let's not let familiarity interfere with God's work in our lives. Let's ask ourselves what changes He wants to make in us today—in our homes, our jobs, our worship, our relationships. Let's not be Gerasenes, but disciples who follow the Master.

PRAYER:

Lord God, we acknowledge you today as our Master, our Leader, our Creator. We know you have a plan for our lives and that your wish for us involves a hope and a future. Please help us to trust you to lead us aright in all areas of our lives, to allow you to make the changes, no matter how drastic and uncomfortable; to shake us out of our familiarity, however strange it may be; and to create in us new and fresh hearts to serve you.

BILLOWING ROBES

...The king took off his signet ring, which he had reclaimed from Haman, and presented it to Mordecai....
"Now write another decree in the king's name in behalf of the Jews as seems best to you, and seal it with the king's signet ring."...
When Mordecai left the king's presence, he was wearing royal garments of blue and white, a large crown of gold and a purple robe of fine linen. And the city of Susa held a joyous celebration.
Esther 8:2, 8, 15 NIV

REFLECTION:

I am fascinated by the book of Esther, not only by the events of the book, but also by the God who arranged them all. Let me briefly fill you in on the situation:

The Jews throughout the vast empire of Persia under Xerxes have been threatened with annihilation. The perpetrator, Haman, does not realize that Queen Esther is a

Jew, or that Mordecai is her cousin and guardian. Through a series of tension-filled scenes, Esther reveals her nationality to King Xerxes and pleads for the lives of her people.

Through another series of divinely orchestrated events, Haman is executed, and Mordecai and Esther are given license to create a new law to supersede the former. Instead of suffering genocide, the Jews of Persia will be allowed to defend themselves and their people, to kill attackers and to plunder their enemies. But the time is short. It could take up to three months for word to reach the ends of the empire.

Mordecai has received power and authority which allow him to carry out the salvation of his people, and I imagine as he leaves the king's presence, dressed in flowing robes of blue and white and purple, he moves with long, purposeful strides, royal robes billowing behind him.

Why do I think so? Mordecai believes he has been called for the specific purpose of saving his people, the Jews. There is no time to waste because the previous edict is still in force (the laws of the Medes and the Persians could not be repealed). He is excited to spread the news, but he and Esther need to create this new law.

Mordecai is one of my heroes. He carries out his job efficiently, he pursues justice (for his people and for the evil Haman), he refuses to bow to society's whims (Haman had ordered him to bow before him), he encourages the frightened to stand up for their faith ("Esther, perhaps you have been brought to this place for such a time as this."), he accepts power and authority with humility and purpose, and he follows through on what he believes.

What are you and I called to do? What is our major definite purpose in life? Are we as determined as Mordecai to do the job before us?

PRAYER:
Oh Lord, we feel the pressures of a godless society all around us. Help us to trust you, striding forward, robes billowing in the determination to follow you, for we are your children and you are our King.

No Bridge to Canaan?

Now the people complained about their hardships in the hearing of the LORD....The rabble with them began to crave other food, and again the Israelites started wailing and said, 'If only we had meat to eat! We remember the fish we ate in Egypt at no cost—also the cucumbers, melons, leeks, onions and garlic. But now we have lost our appetite; we never see anything but this manna!'...
All the Israelites grumbled against Moses and Aaron, and the whole assembly said to them, 'If only...'
Numbers 11:1-6, 14:2 NIV

REFLECTION:

In the book of Numbers, Moses records repeated instances of Israel's grumbling. Life is so hard, they said. We miss the wonderful food of Egypt (how quickly they forgot the whips and hard labor that went with their fine fare). They became insolent towards Moses and Aaron, and ultimately towards God. In His anger and justice, God caused the earth to swallow up the ringleaders, and His fire consumed the 250 power-hungry community leaders, saving only their soot-stained censers. He sent out a plague that killed 14,700 people before it was stopped by Aaron swinging his holy censer. And then—get this—16:41 states: "The next day the whole Israelite community grumbled against Moses and Aaron."

Since it's always easier to point a finger at someone else, let's examine the grumbling of the Hebrews. The people were short on water and food. I imagine I might have complained, too. But God had promised to care for them. In His time, He gave them water, good and sufficient. In His time, He sent them manna, always enough if they followed His instructions, but never more than they needed for each day. They expected Him to provide for them, not because He was Almighty God and they were His chosen people, but because they saw Him as their own personal magician.

They had lost their perspective. God had chosen them as his holy people. He wanted a relationship with them.

I think we have all been disappointed at times, not by God, but in our expectations of him.

Our society strongly suggests that we have all our ducks lined up. Insurance, retirement funds, nest eggs, all those things that make us trust in ourselves. And yet, when our human resources dry up, we grumble and complain that God has forgotten us.

Does God disappoint us? If we expect the future to be cared for today. If we expect all our wants to be supplied. But not if we lean on Him for our daily needs. We must allow Him to direct our lives and bless us in His way and in His time. After all, we belong to Him. He is our Shepherd, our Living Water, our Bread of Life.

Our desert experiences can be teaching times if we're willing to learn. Canaan is just beyond the river. Hmm...I don't see a bridge. I wonder how...

PRAYER:
Dear Father, we thank you for your constant care. Help us to remember that you have our best interests at heart.

SELAH
(Let the reader pause and reflect)

Those who passed by hurled insults at him, shaking their heads and saying, "You who are going to destroy the temple and build it in three days, save yourself! Come down from the cross, if you are the Son of God!"
Matthew 27:39-40 NIV

I and the Father are One.
John 10:30 NIV

Therefore go and make disciples of all nations, baptizing them...and teaching them to obey everything.
I have commanded you. And surely I am with you always, to the very end of the age.
Matthew 28:20 NIV

REFLECTION:

I've just finished re-watching the *Visual Bible's Gospel of Matthew*, portrayed with only the biblical script as dialogue. As always, I'm awed as I watch the Master's life unfold before me. In the final video, Christ is depicted on the cross. I recall reading a quote that it was not the nails that held Christ to the cross; it was love. It was the Father's plan and will before the creation of the world. The Father knew us, how we would fail and fall in spite of everything he showed and taught us, and yet his love could not leave us in Hades. And so he tore his heart by sending his son, Jesus, into the world to take black sin on himself and died in agony for you and for me.

Selah—the writer weeps.

Another part of the Matthew video that has left a lasting impression on me is the very end. Jesus is speaking his last earthly words to his followers, looking each one of them in the eye. Then he looks directly into the camera, and I see God's holy all-consuming love shining from Jesus' eyes. Then he lifts his chin ever so slightly, and in shock, I recognize Almightly God! "I and the Father are one," he has said.

Selah—the writer trembles.

With my heart pounding and my spirit on its face before the Christ, I watch the actor walk away across the sand, and then he turns and beckons me as he beckoned the disciples from their nets, and I wonder if I've ever really considered that I need to leave everything for him.

He walks on and then turns again, this time with a broad smile that speaks of incredible adventure, and waves me to him as if to say, "Hey! Come on already and enjoy my joy." I'm energized and inspired and blessed, and I want to run after him.

And then I realize I must do this every day, this following. What does that mean to me? What does it mean to you?

I think again of the beckoning fingers of the actor portraying Christ and I'm reminded that one day I'll walk off this set with the real Christ, to my heavenly home, and all the disappointments, interruptions and challenges of this life will be nothing in the light of seeing him.

Selah—Even so, come, Lord Jesus.

PRAYER:

My soul is overwhelmed by your majesty and grace, O Christ.

Uplifting Devotionals for Parents

RUTH L. SNYDER

CHURCH TALES

Sunday mornings are rarely the peaceful, worshipful times I would like them to be. They usually start off well, especially when I get up and spend a few quiet minutes reading my Bible and praying. However, once I rouse the rest of the household we start down the slippery Sunday slope.

First there's a mad rush to get dressed. One son can't find matching socks. My youngest daughter complains she's still tired and hides under the covers. Another son puts his dirty clothes on from yesterday after I tell him to put on CLEAN clothes.

Then, there's breakfast. Children squirm and fidget during our family devotions. One of our sons reaches for something and tips over his full glass of milk. Another son refuses to eat because he doesn't like what's on the table.

Next comes the ride to church. We wait for our sixteen-year-old daughter. She gets in and glares because she wasn't allowed to practice driving today. Seat belts are finally on and we're off. Two minutes later, one son is crying because his brother walloped him across the face. When I ask, "Why'd you hit him?" he shrugs. "Hands to yourselves, everyone," I plead. A few minutes later our youngest daughter starts whining that she's thirsty. There are no water bottles in sight. Fortunately the drive to town only lasts ten minutes.

We've made it to church. While I'm catching up with my friends, one of my sons is running laps. I remind him to walk. We resume our conversation. Another son is using the bathroom and forgot to close the door. When we enter the sanctuary, I focus on quieting my heart and mind. That lasts a couple of seconds—until my kids start fighting over who gets to sit beside me. We get the seating arrangement sorted out. Then my youngest son needs to go to the bathroom. He's sitting the farthest from the aisle and trips over someone's foot on his way out. Now his nose is bleeding. I rush him to the bathroom where I discover splatters of blood all the way down his brand new shirt. We clean up the best we can and return to the sanctuary. Again, I try to calm myself and focus on what God wants to teach me.

Sometimes I grasp most of the Pastor's message; many times I don't. But I've come to love and accept Sunday mornings with my imperfect kids and my even more imperfect parenting. After all, God doesn't love me because I'm perfect; He loves me because He chooses to love me.

I've discovered that some of life's greatest lessons are taught not by what happens, but by how I respond in messy situations. I've also found peace in the midst of the turbulence of raising five challenging children, because God's strength is made perfect in my weakness. Here are some choices that help me cope:

1. Celebrate the "gifts" I receive every day, no matter how insignificant. (e.g. My washing machine works, I'm alive, The sunset is beautiful)

2. Acknowledge that I cannot successfully do anything without God

3. Spend time reading the Bible and praying

4. Remind myself that God is always with me and talk to Him about my joys and frustrations throughout the day

5. Share my journey with other women who will be brutally honest with me

Prayer: Father, Thank you that you understand the challenges of parenting. Help me to rely on your wisdom and strength today in all I do and say. Amen

A TIME FOR EVERYTHING

When was the last time you had one of "those days?" You know, when your attention is torn in twenty different directions and you literally race from one event to the next, often arriving breathless ... and late. A while back I had too many of "those days" in succession, and I prayed that God would show me what I needed to keep in my schedule and what needed to go.

It's healthy to take a look at our goals every once in a while. As parents we have many demands on our time; the reality is that we can't do everything and do it well.

Ecclesiastes 3:1 (NASB) says, "There is **an appointed time** for everything. And there is **a time** for every event under heaven." Note that it doesn't say, "There is time for everything." Verses 2-8 list many experiences common to mankind, such as birth and death, planting and harvesting. Verse 9 asks a question we all ask at one time or another, "What profit is there to the worker from that in which he toils?" In other words, what's the point? Verses 11-14 provide the answer – God's gift to us is satisfaction in our work and our choice to "rejoice and do good in one's life."

As I've considered how best to make use of the limited time God gives me, the following questions have been helpful:

1. What life stage (e.g. single, couple, married with young kids, retired) am I living and what realities go along with that stage?

2. What are my spiritual gifts and how can I use them to serve others (see I Peter 4:10)? What brings joy to my heart and makes me feel energized?

3. How do I currently use my time? What priorities are reflected by the way I use my time? What do I need to change?

4. If I knew I only had one year to live from today, what would I most like to accomplish?

5. What "urgent" tasks often derail me from doing what's important? ("The more important, the less likely it is urgent; the more urgent, the less likely it is important." General Eisenhower)

6. Are these my plans, or God's plans? If these are God's plans and He allows what I consider to be an interruption, then I should be willing to adjust and carry on. ("Sometimes we are so stubborn that the only way God can get through to us is with a crisis." Mark Porter)

Life doesn't have to be insanely busy to be productive. I'm still sifting through priorities and setting goals, but I've made adjustments already. Will you join me?

Helpful Resources:
"Biblical Priorities – The Christlike Lifestyle."
http://www.resources4discipleship.com/mediafiles/Biblical-Priorities.pdf
"How to Use Time Well."
http://www.rogerdarlington.me.uk/Time.html
Hummel, Charles. *Priorities: Tyranny of the Urgent*

Porter, Mark. *The Time of Your Life: How to Accomplish All that God Wants You to Do*

"Spiritual Gifts Bible Teaching for Christians."
http://mintools.com/discovergifts.htm

TerKeurst, Lysa. *The Best Yes: Making Wise Decisions in the Midst of Endless Demands*

Prayer: Father, thank you that you have given me specific gifts and talents to serve You and others. Help me to be faithful in using the time that You give me today. Amen.

The Rush to the Bus

One day when I told Levi to make his lunch, he ignored me and kept playing. I set the timer and again instructed him to get his lunch made. This time he came out of his room and threw a few choice words my way.

"Levi, you have five minutes to make your sandwich. If you don't, I'll put a roast beef sandwich in your lunch kit for you." (He is particular about his lunches and does NOT like roast beef sandwiches.)

With a minute to spare, his sandwich was in his lunch kit. His older sister even had him smiling and singing along to a silly song from a Paddington Bear movie.

As soon as I showed up with Levi's hearing aids, the smile vanished. He covered both ears with his hands.

"Levi, why don't you want your hearing aids in today?"

No response.

I lifted his hand off his left ear and immediately an elbow took its place. "Levi, I need you to tell me why you don't want your hearing aids in."

Still no response. I remembered the school was having some issues with his FM system – more than one piece of equipment on the same radio frequency, resulting in Levi hearing instructions from another classroom. "You need to wear one hearing aid today. Your right one doesn't have the FM on it. How about if I put that one in for you?"

He peeked at me, still not totally convinced. However, he did allow me to put the right hearing aid in.

"Time for jackets!"

Four kids raced for jackets. Levi marched to his room.

I helped my youngest daughter and then went looking for Levi. He was still in his room. As I entered, Levi hit the floor, crawling under the bed. I caught him and sat him on my lap. "Buddy, it's time to go to school."

He shook his head.

All morning he had been telling me by his actions that he didn't want to go to school. Time was ticking. I knew the bus was coming. What should I do?

I shot up a quick prayer, and then told Levi we needed to go to the bus.

He walked beside me, silent.

Ahead of us the other children frolicked and played. A few minutes later the bus pulled up. I hugged Levi and glanced at his face. Tears dripped off his chin, but he marched onto the bus.

My heart was heavy as I turned back towards the house. "Lord, did I do the right thing today? Thank you that you're with Levi. Please help him to have a good day."

Fortunately, this story has a happy ending. Levi came home all excited about a new project at school. Whew!

Getting kids out the door to the bus every morning can be challenging enough for most families. However, when kids have special needs, the challenge is even greater; we perform a delicate dance each day – taking into account the individual needs of each child while also making sure necessary tasks are accomplished.

Perhaps you have a friend who has a child with special needs. Here are some ways my friends help me:

1. Ask how you can pray for your friend and her child.

2. Provide a listening ear. Sometimes your friend may just need to vent.

3. Learn about the child's special needs. If you feel comfortable and have the required skills, offer to provide respite for your friend so he or she can do something he or she enjoys.

Father, thank you for the gift of children with special needs and that they help us better understand your amazing love. Give me the strength and patience I need to reach out to those around me who are dealing with the challenges special needs present. Amen.

6 Ways to Help Children Develop a Personal Relationship with Jesus Christ

Parenting is one of the most challenging jobs I've ever faced. These little bundles I hold in my arms for a few short years need to be fed, nurtured, and taught. There's food to make, clothes to wash, life skills to teach, books to read, homework to monitor, chores to organize, games to play, and the list goes on. Sometimes I'm overwhelmed by it all.

Deuteronomy 6, says:

"5 Love the LORD your God with all your heart and with all your soul and with all your strength. 6 These commandments that I give you today are to be on your hearts. 7 Impress them on your children. Talk about them when you sit at home and when you walk along the road, when you lie down and when you get up. 8 Tie them as symbols on your hands and bind them on your foreheads. 9 Write them on the door-frames of your houses and on your gates." (NIV)

Here are some ways I'm teaching my children about God:

1. **Maintain a personal quiet time** – I need to nurture my own walk with God in order to effectively teach my children to do the same. When my children were young, I found it most effective to have a short Bible reading like Our Daily Bread (http://odb.org/) that I could read quickly. Now that my children are older, I get up early so I can be by myself to read my Bible, sing, and pray.

2. **Have devotions together as a family** – The best way to teach something is to do it together. My husband and I make family devotions a priority by reading the Bible and praying together with our children before we have breakfast. We use a variety of resources including reading a Psalm or

Proverb every day or reading devotionals from Focus on the Family. (http://shop.focusonthefamily.ca/Parenting/Faith-at-Home/).

3. **Pray with children before school** – Every morning while we are waiting for the bus to arrive, I pray with my children, committing their day to God and asking for protection, wisdom, and help in making the right choices.

4. **Use teachable moments** – If we are alert to them, teachable moments are available to us almost every day. These opportunities could be as simple as asking for a child's forgiveness when I act inappropriately, or pointing out something in God's amazing creation and talking about God's character and attributes.

5. **Verbalize thankfulness** – Often I tend to take things for granted. My attitude and the attitudes of my children change when I verbalize thankfulness. "Remember when we prayed for ...? See how God answered? Let's thank Him!" Or "What a beautiful sunrise! Thank you, God, for a new day!"

6. **Attend Church as a family** – Hebrews 10:25 says:

"23 Let us hold unswervingly to the hope we profess, for he who promised is faithful. 24 And let us consider how we may spur one another on toward love and good deeds, 25 not giving up meeting together, as some are in the habit of doing, but encouraging one another—and all the more as you see the Day approaching." (NIV)

There may be other ways that you can think of. The most important thing is to be intentional and make these actions part of our schedule.

Prayer: Father, thank you that you have given me the responsibility of being a parent. Help me to be faithful in teaching my children about You and living a life that is pleasing to you. Amen.

Adoption: A Glimpse into the Heart of God

Have you ever noticed how certain passages of Scripture come alive in a new way because of what you're experiencing in your personal life? One morning during our family Bible reading, my husband read from Galatians:

"*23 Before the coming of this faith, we were held in custody under the law, locked up until the faith that was to come would be revealed. 24 So the law was our guardian until Christ came that we might be justified by faith. 25 Now that this faith has come, we are no longer under a guardian.*

26 So in Christ Jesus you are all children of God through faith, 27 for all of you who were baptized into Christ have clothed yourselves with Christ. 28 There is neither Jew nor Gentile, neither slave nor free, nor is there male and female, for you are all one in Christ Jesus. 29 If you belong to Christ, then you are Abraham's seed, and heirs according to the promise.

(Chapter 4) What I am saying is that as long as an heir is underage, he is no different from a slave, although he owns the whole estate. 2 The heir is subject to guardians and trustees until the time set by his father. 3 So also, when we were underage, we were in slavery under the elemental spiritual forces of the world. 4 But when the set time had fully come, God sent his Son, born of a woman, born under the law, 5 to redeem those under the law, that we might receive **adoption to sonship**. *6 Because you are his sons, God sent the Spirit of his Son into our hearts, the Spirit who calls out, "Abba, Father." 7 So you are no longer a slave, but God's child; and since you are his child, God has made you also an heir.*" (**Galatians** 3:23-4:7 NIV)

I've read this passage many times before. I knew that I used to be a prisoner to sin, that the law showed me my need of a Savior, etc. However, I had never stopped to think about the rights and privileges God granted me when he ADOPTED me into His family.

My husband and I have had the privilege of adopting five children. They came to us at different ages, through various circumstances, with unique needs. However, before we adopted them, they were all orphans. They had no one committed to caring for them for life. When we adopted them, they gained a permanent home, love, hope for the future, committed advocates, an inheritance, and a family name.

Adoption is a beautiful glimpse into the heart of God. He loved us so much that He was willing to make the ultimate sacrifice of Jesus Christ's death on the cross to pay the penalty for our sin. When we accept His free gift of salvation, He provides His presence every day, an eternal home in heaven, perfect love, incredible hope, an advocate (the Holy Spirit), an inheritance out of this world, and an amazing family (the Church). Isn't that wonderful?

Prayer: Father, thank you for the way adoption gives us a glimpse into Your heart. Help me today to rejoice in the blessings you've given to me as your adopted child. Amen.

I LOVE YOU

One day I was sitting in a wooden rocking chair with my one-year-old daughter. She sat facing me, laughing and giggling as we played Pat a Cake and Round and Round the Garden. Her laughter was infectious. I wrapped my arms around her and said, "I love you." She smiled up at me, her big blue eyes sparkling, wrapped her chubby arms around my neck and said, "I wuv oo." We repeated the action and words over and over, smiling and laughing until the tears dripped off our cheeks.

One of the things I enjoy about toddlers is their spontaneity and fun-loving spirits. They are like little sponges, learning by imitation. The quality of their learning is dependent on the caregivers they interact with. Unfortunately, these little people pick up bad habits just as easily as they learn good ones.

The phrase, "I love you," is overused in our society and has lost some of its meaning. It's easy to say the words, but it's more difficult to demonstrate our love consistently. As a parent, we experience delightful times with our children, like the one I described above. This is good. However, what happens when we are exhausted and our child is whining or screaming at us? Or when our child has the flu and throws up in the middle of the night, the third time in a couple hours? Or when our child stomps his foot and refuses to do what we ask?

I John 4:7-10 says:
"7 Dear friends, let us love one another, for love comes from God. Everyone who loves has been born of God and knows God. 8 Whoever does not love does not know God, because God is love. 9 This is how God showed his love among us: He sent his one and only Son into the world that we might live through him. 10 This is love: not that we loved God, but that he loved us and sent his Son as an atoning sacrifice for our sins." (NIV)

God is the one who teaches us about true love, not just by what He says, but also by what He does for us. His love is dependable, not fickle. Our society treats love as if it's a feeling that fades over time; something to be enjoyed while it lasts and then thrown away. This is not the love God demonstrates. Love is a choice.

When life is tough and parenting is a struggle, we need to choose to love anyway. When we are exhausted and our child is screaming at us, we need to rely on God for strength, bite our tongue and gently deal with him or her. If he is tired or hungry, the best thing to do is ignore the behaviour and meet his physical needs. When our daughter throws up in the middle of the night, again, we must trust God for strength and wash our child and the bedding (separately, of course!). When our son stomps his foot and refuses to do what we ask, we must gently remind him that God made us his parent and hand out consequences instead of reacting out of anger.

We are human and will make mistakes in our parenting. However, if we make it our aim to consistently love our children, they will learn to trust us. Hopefully, they will also learn to trust God as their loving Heavenly Father as well.

Prayer: Father, help me to be consistent in my parenting in easy times and difficult times. You know that I'm human. Give me the strength to be the parent You want me to be. Amen.

CHOOSING MY FOCUS

The other day I spent most of my waking hours doing laundry—eight loads of smelly, dirty clothes—between other household responsibilities like making meals, keeping kids on task while doing chores, and reading a story or two. The first load consisted of sheets and a mattress cover from one of my son's beds. Later that day, I folded the lemon-scented clothes while my children washed the grime of summer play away in the bathtub. It was a relief to fold the last pair of pyjamas. Now I just had to put the clean clothes away, and then I was done for the day.

I grabbed a mountain of clothing from among the piles on our dining room table and marched into our sons' bedroom. Smiling, I passed the first bed with its freshly laundered sheets. And stopped dead in my tracks. The sparkling white sheets were sprinkled with light brown in several places. Sand! As my teeth ground together in frustration, God spoke to me.

"What are you going to focus on? A few temporary sprinkles of sand or the permanent character of your son?"

"But I just washed those sheets!"

"Yes, I know. But in the grand scheme of things, what are a few grains of sand?"

Deuteronomy 4:9 says, "Only be careful, and watch yourselves closely so that you do not forget the things your eyes have seen or let them fade from your heart as long as you live. Teach them to your children and to their children after them." (NIV)

There are many times in the daily grind of caring for my kids when I need to be very careful and watchful. It only took a few seconds to sweep those grains of sand off my son's bed. It would have been easy to react in anger, but a few careless words expressing my frustration could have caused damage to my relationship with my son for years to come. When I get busy and think of things only from my perspective, small things get blown way out of proportion.

One thing that helps me keep perspective is to remember what God has done for me in the past, how He has dealt with me in mercy and compassion. I've done foolish things, but God has forgiven me. Can I do any less for my son?

Parents need to teach children many things. Yes, my children need to learn to dress themselves, clean their rooms, comb their hair, etc. However, my top priority is teaching my children about God and preparing the soil of their hearts to have a personal relationship with Him. Cultivating an awareness of and openness to God takes time and energy.

Children learn best when they see faith lived out by me personally. My children are all too aware of my frailty and failures. When I do mess up, the best thing I can do is be honest with them, confess my sin to them, and ask for forgiveness.

I'm still learning to choose my focus, daily, hourly, even each minute of the day. I'm thankful God walks with me and speaks to me. Now if I could only learn to listen better.

Prayer: Father, thank you that You walk through each day with me. Help me to listen to Your still, small voice so that I can be the parent you want me to be for my children. Amen.

Critiquing Canticles

TONY HILLING

DAY 1

"My soul magnifies the Lord,
and my spirit has rejoiced in God my Saviour"
Luke 1:47

As a young boy 12 years old, I left my home in Scotland and went to a Roman Catholic seminary in the north of England. At that time the liturgy of the RC church was still done completely in Latin. Every Sunday evening at the conclusion of Vespers (Evening Prayer), we would sing the Canticle of Mary. Now, more than fifty years later, I can still hear in my heart the beautiful tones of the Gregorian Chant: "Magnificat anima mea Dominum."

Mary's Canticle was reported to us originally in Greek. But her first two phrases still reveal a characteristic of Hebrew poetry: a couplet which simply states the same idea twice. A similar example would be the opening of Psalm 103. *"Bless the Lord, O my soul; and all that is within me, bless His holy name."*

The intention of the original writer is then to hit the main idea twice. Therefore, Psalm 103:1 and Luke 1:46 are saying essentially the same thing: praise and worship the Lord God with the very core of our being.

The context of the Canticle is a conversation between two women who had good reason to praise God: the previously barren Elizabeth was now carrying God's messenger; Mary was carrying His only Son. But not only this, there has been a great absence of revelation from God over the past four hundred years. Some ancient commentators called it the Four Hundred Years of Silence. And now God is speaking very loudly indeed, more reason to praise Him. But do we praise God only when we have a clear reason to rejoice in something?

For the Christian there is something normative about praise of God; it must be done daily regardless of the circumstances. I remember listening to a message by Allan

Vincent, a British missionary then resident in the U.S. He shared with us that in the Holy Land they have two main types of figs: the summer figs and the winter figs. The summer figs are planted in the Spring and harvested in the Fall. They are the fruit of the warm season and can be insipid. The winter figs are planted in the Fall and harvested in the Spring. They have to endure the cold season in the Holy Land. These figs are firm and juicy.

We must praise God daily in our lives, but especially in the difficult times for then it is real praise. Our praise of God becomes like the winter figs. The prophet Habakkuk echos this attitude at 3:17 &18, where he writes that though there be no fruit on the vines or figs or olive trees, nor any cattle in the stall,
"...Yet, I will exult in the Lord, I will rejoice in the God of my salvation." Such an attitude of mind bespeaks faith, trust and devotion to God beyond whatever He can do for us. It was Mary's attitude; it must become ours.

DAY 2

"For He has regarded the lowly state of His maidservant;
For behold, henceforth all generations will call me blessed"
Luke 1:48

When Harry Truman was thrust into the presidency by the death of Franklin Delano Roosevelt, Sam Rayburn took him aside.
"From here on out you're going to have lots of people around you. They'll try to put up a wall around you and cut you off from any ideas but theirs. They'll tell you what a great man you are, Harry. But you and I both know you ain't."[i]
Sam Rayburn may have forgotten about this incident, but I'm sure Harry Truman never did. The story probably came from him. If it did, it would have been a mark in his favour: a man and a president that had a healthy self evaluation and a sense of humour as well.

Mary's self evaluation is equally blunt. She rejoices that God has regarded with kindness her lowliness, she who was His female slave. In saying this she speaks from a great tradition of biblical writers who affirm that the God of Israel had a preferential love for the people of little account. It is almost as if the spirit of the true Israel never quite forgot the slavery of their past. However this skeleton in their closet turned out to be one of the greatest treasures that they passed on to believers in the New Testament. The humble, poor and afflicted, or the "Anawim", as they came to be called, were the very ones who had best understood "...their own helplessness and utter dependence on God."[ii]

This insight is not captured easily by us. We, people of the western world are such a generation of planners and schemers that the most basic truth of our complete dependence on Almighty God has eluded us. We are a culture that has cast an idol of our own wits, blessed all the more religiously by our perfunctory prayers. Some of our churches have even led the way in effective humanism. Must we await the arrival of the Tribulation to convince us of our spiritual ineptitude (with all apologies to those who believe we will be raptured first)?

Mary grasped her own state before God and it was no false humility for in the next breath she declares that all generations would call her blessed; a statement that would be proved prophetic. This humble maiden of Nazareth was not afraid to boast in the Lord. As her Son so eloquently put it, "...everyone who exalts himself will be humbled and he who humbles himself will be exalted." (Luke 18:14).

DAY 3

"For He who is mighty has done great things for me,
And Holy is His name."

Luke 1:49

A number of years ago I took a leave from ministry and decided to go back to my original career of practising law. The transition was difficult for me and I began to drag my feet at the task of requalifying. An older friend who was also a lawyer rebuked me for my tardiness and told me that I had to "make things happen." As we would say today, "No pressure!" I don't know about you, but when I begin to make things happen I start to get into trouble and go back to my old habits of sin. Michael Dye, an addictions counsellor with over thirty years experience wrote a workbook entitled, "The Genesis Process",[iii] which challenges Christians to make the transforming journey into personal change. In Process 15 of his work, he writes of "the Faster Scale"[iv], a six stage downward spiral leading to relapse. The advantage of perceiving this is of course to allow interventions that arrest us from falling back. "Making things happen" would put me squarely on the Faster Scale.

Mary's words show her as one of the lowly, the *"Anawim"*: those who depended totally on God. She didn't need to make things happen. The Almighty made things happen for her. And yet she still had a clear sense of His transcendence. *"...and holy is His name."* So it was not as if she had assumed "buddy" status with the Lord. She recognized that she was one of the poor. Yet precisely because of this she also knew that she could trust in Him. So, her confidence in Him and her knowledge that He was infinitely above her went hand in hand.

The reverse is true in our culture. We are self-made men and women, and perhaps because of that very reason, we have lost our sense of the holy. Put us under pressure and our immediate response is to problem-solve. Now I am not advocating passivity or a refusal to engage in the normal activities of our society. But let's make sure that our 'get 'er done' attitude and our technological prowess have not stolen our biblical mindset. Regardless of the achievements of Western Civilization, we were lost until the Father sent us His Only Son to die for our sins. And there was absolutely nothing we could have done about our natural state of being cut off from Him. As I am fond of saying to my congregation, if we could have saved ourselves, we would have done it already! In the twentieth century alone there were three major genocides by the three major racial types: Europeans, Asians and Africans. And that was just the major genocides. What does that tell us about ourselves? We have a virus! The bible calls it

Sin. We desperately need our God. Making things happen would just make things worse.

I pray for the day when the men and women of this planet will return to the God revealed in the Bible. It will start when believers reclaim these truths that found a home in Mary's heart: confidence in His might alone; in awe of His holiness.

DAY 4

"And His mercy is from age to age
On those who fear Him."

Luke 1:50

Have you ever noticed how counter-cultural the Bible is? Some of its statements really bug us, perhaps every culture but especially our own. An example is the above statement. As I consider who we have become, I've observed that we really like what we call a level playing field. We don't like it when people adopt an attitude of superiority, or even when our leaders get too far ahead of us. Perhaps this is a reaction against some of the examples of the very sharp class distinctions in our histories. The word, "mercy" has aromas of condescension and of certain folks being inferior by the very fact that they need mercy. A word-picture might be an ancient tale where one conquering party has a sword at the throat of another conquered party and demands that the latter beg for mercy. That sense of the word mercy does not leave us with a warm, comfortable feeling. It is not what we would call a popular word today. And "fear", well that's even worse!

As you would probably guess, the Bible uses these words, "mercy" and "fear" in quite distinct ways that are important for us to grasp. "Mercy" is a word that describes beautifully and accurately God's overtures to the human race throughout history: a holy, almighty and unapproachable God draws near and offers forgiveness and new life to the very ones who have offended Him deeply.

The heart of mercy is God's compassion for us by which He passes over the wrongs we have done to Him; mercy by its nature is undeserved. Mary spoke of God's mercy being,

"...from generation to generation." We read in a number of Psalms about God being rich in mercy and slow to anger. We might remember the stories in the Book of Judges where the Israelites turned away from God time after time, yet when they repented, He forgave them. The Holy Scriptures are full of examples of God's mercy. But the best example is the Son of God setting aside His divinity, becoming a man like us, and carrying all or sins to the cross so that we would enjoy eternal life with Him. This is mercy, indeed!

But did not Luke have Mary say that God's mercy is for those who fear Him? Shouldn't she have said it for those who love Him? In fact, biblical 'fear of the Lord' goes hand in hand with love of the Lord. The 'fear of the Lord' is a biblical term that means that we are so caught up in our love of the Lord that we have a holy dread of grieving Him or even disappointing Him, through sin. It is a real fear. Isaiah 11:3 speaks of the Holy Spirit resting on the Messiah who will delight in the fear of the Lord. The fear of the Lord is then linked closely with an abhorrence of sin.

God's mercy is for those who fear Him. In a sense, His mercy is conditional on human repentance that includes a holy fear. Of course, we have a choice to reject God's mercy, and so face His justice. To do so would be to face another kind of fear that is not holy at all. Perhaps you remember that scene in Star Wars where Luke Skywalker says to Yoda, "I am not afraid." Yoda's response is, "You will be!" As we are fond of saying today, "Don't go there!" But for those who have accepted God's mercy in holy fear, they stand in the righteousness of the only Son of God. Their destiny is eternal life.

DAY 5

"He has shown strength with His arm;
He has scattered the proud
In the imagination of their hearts"

I remember reading a story in the Reader's Digest of August, 1979, about a man who lived in Dublin who was named, Anthony S. Clancy. He was born on the seventh day of the seventh month in 1907 and was the seventh son of a seventh son, which in Irish tradition indicated that the person had great psychic ability. Armed with his special powers, he went to the races on his 27th birthday and put all his money (seven pounds) on a horse called "Seventh Heaven". The horse came in seventh!

My heritage is at least three quarters Irish and this story always makes me smile. I suppose in a whimsical way it illustrates God resisting the proud (<u>James 4:6; 1 Peter 5:5</u>). However the line from the Canticle of Mary says more. God not only resists the proud, but scatters them. Losing your money at the races would be a good example of your pride being scattered! But why does God do this? I believe that it is all about God manifesting His Sovereignty. In this respect the NKJ version's of God "showing" strength with His arm is accurate. God doesn't just do mighty things, but He reveals the strength of His Godhead in so doing. God has a track record of manifesting Himself as God: as infinitely superior to humanity, particularly fallen humanity. And yet because of our "fallenness", we naturally desire to assert our independence, our plans and our perspective that we must be free from His interference in our lives. The Bible calls this the "imagination of our hearts". We imagine that we are something, when we are not. The truth is, folks, that we think a little too much of ourselves, and God must take us down a peg for our own good.

However God is not doing this because He, "has issues", or because He was dropped as a baby. He is not petulantly asserting His rights as God. He literally must show us who He is and who we are. <u>Proverbs 16:18</u> reads, "Pride goes before destruction, and a haughty spirit before a fall." Do we want to fall? Worse, do we want to walk the road to destruction? Because pride will get us there handily. The Dawkins's and the Hawking's of this world did not arrive at their present destination through some grand scientific thesis: Q.E.D. there is no God! It is simply human pride refusing to believe. What a fearful thing to lay our ladder against a wall, climb up most of the way and find that we laid it against the wrong wall. And frequently, our pride prevents us from going back.

But God wants us to go back; He's a saving God. When He scatters the proud in the imagination of their hearts, it is so that they might have a change of heart and turn to Him. He scatters so that He might one day gather us to Himself.

He's our Father and He wants us to make it safely home; and Jesus is the Way. But to take that road, we must abandon our pride. If pride comes before destruction, humbling ourselves will lead us to salvation.

---

[i] "1001 Quotes, Illustrations and Humorous Stories", Edward K. Rowell & Leadership, ed., BakerBooks, 2008, p.259.

[ii] The Interpreter's Dictionary of the Bible, E-J, G.A. Buttrick et al, ed., "Humility", G. E. Mendenhall, p.659, Abingdon Press, Nashville, 1985.

[iii] Dye, Michael, CADC, NCAC II, "The Genesis Process", 4th Edition, 2012,

[iv] Ibid pp. 233, 237

Made in the USA
Charleston, SC
12 February 2015